D1619034

POWER PRESSURE COOKER XL COOKBOOK

------- ❧❦❧❦ -------

Step By Step Guide For Healthy, Easy And Delicious Electric Pressure Recipes

John Carter

TABLE OF CONTENTS

INTRODUCTION 10

CHAPTER ONE 11

    ABOUT THE POWER PRESSURE COOKER XL 11

CHAPTER TWO 13

    HOW TO USE THE POWER PRESSURE
    COOKER XL 13

CHAPTER THREE 16

    PRESSURE COOKER MUSHROOM MARSALA
    SOUP 16

CHAPTER FOUR 19

    PRESSURE COOKER CRANBERRY BAKED
    FRENCH TOAST 19

CHAPTER FIVE 22

    TASTY CRANBERRY APPLE SAUCE 22

CHAPTER SIX 24

    JAPANESE PRESSURE COOKER BEEF CURRY 24

CHAPTER SEVEN 28

    BABY BACK RIBS 28

CHAPTER EIGHT 30

    RED BEANS AND RICE 30

CHAPTER NINE 32

    MINI RIGATONESE BOLOGNESE 32

CHAPTER TEN 34

    PRESSURE COOKER STUFFED GREEN PEPPER
    CASSEROLE 34

CHAPTER ELEVEN 36

    PRESSURE COOKER GREEN CHILE PORK
    CARNITAS 36

CHAPTER TWELVE 39

    PRESSURE COOKER CRUSTLESS TOMATO
    SPINACH QUICHE 39

CHAPTER THIRTEEN 41

    CHOCOLATE POT DE CREME 41

CHAPTER FOURTEEN 43

    PRESSURE COOKER SMOKY HAM HOCK AND
    PINTO BEAN SOUP 43

CHAPTER FIFTEEN 45

    PRESSURE COOKER KOREAN CHICKEN THIGHS 45

CHAPTER SIXTEEN 48

    PRESSURE COOKER VEGETABLE BEEF AND
    RICE SOUP 48

CHAPTER SEVENTEEN 50

    PRESSURE COOKER ORANGE CHICKEN 50

CHAPTER EIGHTEEN...52

    PRESSURE COOKER PULLED PORK.........................52

CHAPTER NINETEEN...56

    LOADED INSTANT POT MAC AND CHEESE.............56

CHAPTER TWENTY...60

    NEW YORK INSTANT POT CHEESE CAKE................60

CHAPTER TWENTY ONE..66

    PRESSURE COOKER BEEF STROGANOFF................66

CHAPTER TWENTY TWO...68

    TABOULI SALAD..68

CHAPTER TWENTY THREE...70

    SWEET POTATO...70

CHAPTER TWENTY FOUR...72

    THAI PEANUT NOODLE..72

CHAPTER TWENTY FIVE..74

    PRESSURE COOKER SPAGHETTI SQUASH..............74

CHAPTER TWENTY SIX..76

    PICADILLO..76

CHAPTER TWENTY SEVEN..78

    PEACH AND CHERRY COMPOTE............................78

CHAPTER TWENTY EIGHT..80

MEXICAN STREET CORN..80

CHAPTER TWENTY NINE 82

LENTIL SOUP 82

CHAPTER TWENTY NINE 84

INSTANT POT TERIYAKI CHICKEN AND RICE 84

CHAPTER THIRTY..87

BBQ INSTANT POT RIBS 87

CHAPTER THIRTY ONE.. 89

PRESSURE COOKER CHAR SIU (CHINESE BBQ
PORK) 89

CHAPTER THIRTY TWO 92

PRESSURE COOKER PORK CHOPS IN HK
TOMATO SAUCE.. 92

CHAPTER THIRTY THREE 96

PRESSURE COOKER CHICKEN CONGEE................... 96

CHAPTER THIRTY FOUR 98

PRESSURE COOKER CREAMY ENCHILADA SOUP... 98

CHAPTER FIVE 101

PRESSURE COOKER HONEY SESAME CHICKEN 101

CHAPTER THIRTY SIX..103

PRESSURE COOKER MEATBALLS IN EASY
TOMATO SAUCE..103

CHAPTER THIRTY SEVEN 106

    POTATO LEEK SOUP 106

CHAPTER THIRTY EIGHT 108

    SOUTHERN SAUSAGE GRAVY 108

CHAPTER THIRTY NINE.................................110

    AVOCADO CHICKEN SOUP 110

CHAPTER FORTY 112

    SLOPPY JOES 112

CHAPTER FORTY-ONE.....................................114

    CIOPPINO 114

CHAPTER FORTY TWO 116

    PUMPKIN SPICE RISOTTO 116

CHAPTER FORTY THREE 118

    POMEGRANATE LEG OF LAMB 118

CHAPTER FORTY FOUR.................................... 120

    LOADED MASHED POTATOES 120

CHAPTER FORTY FIVE 122

    GLAZED CARROT 122

CHAPTER FORTY SIX 124

    PRESSURE COOKER BBQ WINGS 124

CHAPTER FORTY SEVEN.................................. 126

MOIST AND TENDER PRESSURE COOKER
TURKEY BREAST 126

CHAPTER FORTY EIGHT 128

PRESSURE COOKER PUMPKIN CRÈME BRÛLÉE....128

CHAPTER FORTY NINE 131

PRESSURE COOKER TURKEY STOCK 131

CHAPTER FIFTY 133

PRESSURE COOKER DATE BROWN RICE
PUDDING 133

CHAPTER FIFTY ONE 135

PRESSURE COOKER STUFFING.............................. 135

CHAPTER FIFTY TWO....................................... 137

PRESSURE COOKER BUTTERNUT SQUASH
BUTTER.. 137

INTRODUCTION

The Power Pressure Cooker XL will make your cooking very easy!

Cooking has in no way been easier with the Power Pressure Cooker XL. The Power Pressure Cooker XL is very efficient — using the power pressure of steam to cook so fast and so luxuriously. With only a push of a button, you get to prepare all your favorite delicacies with all of their minerals and vitamins locked in them.

From sautéing, stewing and steaming to canning, slow cooking, warming and lots more, the Power Pressure Cooker XL, with its One-Touch Preset Buttons, Pre-Programmed Smart Settings and Flavor Infusion Technology has been designed to make cooking a fast and incredibly enjoyable experience.

In this book are delicious electric power pressure cooker recipes that include breakfast, brunch, beef, pork, poultry, pork, vegetables, seafood, stews, soups, desserts and more. Meat and seafood cooked in Your Power Pressure Cooker XL will retain their intense flavor without extra fat; vegetables also come out tender-crisp, with their fiber in one piece. For people who love to eat nutritious home-cooked meals, this book is created for you!

What then are you waiting for? Cook delicious meals in your Power Pressure Cooker XL Today!

CHAPTER ONE

ABOUT THE POWER PRESSURE COOKER XL

The Power Pressure Cooker XL is a digital pressure cooker that says it is a "one button, one pot kitchen miracle" helping you to prepare all of your most preferred slow-cooked meals in a fraction of the time.

Due to this, the Power Pressure Cooker XL claims to help you prepare succulent, wholesome meals with just one touch of a button and up to 70% faster than the conventional methods, saving you more time, energy, and money.

You can prepare your favorite slow-cooked recipes 70% faster and make one-pot meals with just a touch of a button with the Electric Power Pressure Cooker XL. It features flavor infusion technology that helps lock in flavor and nutrients for tasty and healthier results.

- Electric Power Pressure Cooker XL lets you cook delicious, flavorful and healthier meals up to 70% faster than traditional cookware and is also good for canning fruits, vegetables, and more

- Intelligent one touch preset options makes room for you to perfectly cook meat, fish, vegetables, beans, rice, soup or stews with just a press of a button

- Flavor infusion technology keeps super heated steam inside the pot to force liquid and moisture into your food, locking in strong flavor and nutrients

- Push-button control panel with digital display

- Slow cooker function without stress and perfectly makes your favorite slow-cooked recipes 10x faster

- Safe lock lid with manual steam release

- Manual pressure and cooking time adjustments

- Automatic keep warm mode

- Large and sturdy lid arm handle

CHAPTER TWO

HOW TO USE THE POWER PRESSURE COOKER XL

All the pressure cooker buttons cook in the same manner except the canning button. So it doesn't matter which button you use, just chose the button with the closest cook time to the time in the recipe you want to cook.

The Power Pressure Cooker XL pressure buttons:

- Fish/Vegetables/Steam – 2 minute cook time. With the cook time selector, adjust your cook time to 4 or 10 minutes. This is the shortest cook time available on the Power Pressure Cooker XL

- Beans/Lentils – 5 minute cook time. Use the cook time selector to adjust your cook time to 15 or 30 minutes.

- Rice/Risotto – 6 minute cook time. Use the cook time selector to adjust to 18 or 25 minutes. The manual recommends using 6 minutes for white rice, 18 minutes for brown rice, and 25 minutes for wild rice.

- Soup/Stew – 10 minute cook time. Use the cook time selector to adjust the cook time to 30 or 60 minutes.

- Rice/Risotto – 6 minute cook time, use the cook time selector to adjust to 18 or 25 minutes. The manual recommends using 6 minutes for white rice, 18 minutes for brown rice, and 25 minutes for wild rice.

- Soup/Stew – 10 minute cook time, use the cook time selector to adjust to 30 or 60 minutes.

- Meat/Chicken – 15 minute cook time, use the cook time selector to adjust to 40 or 60 minutes.

Additional Power Pressure Cooker XL buttons:

- Canning – the canning button cooks at 12 psi, which is high pressure in the Instant Pot. If you please, you can do all your pressure cooking with the canning button if you're pressure cooking longer than 10 minutes. You can regulate the time to 45 and 120 minutes. The Power Pressure Cooker manual does not suggest pressure canning if you are at an altitude above 2,000 ft. However, a division of the USDA warned consumers against pressure canning in digital (electric) pressure cookers. Hot water bath canning is harmless

- Slow Cook – 2 hour cook time. Use the cook time selector to adjust to 6 hours or 12 hours.

- Keep Warm/Cancel Button – Use this button to cancel a function or turn off your pressure cooker. When you pressure cooking time is up, it will automatically switch to Keep Warm.

- Delay Timer – This lets you set the pressure cooker to start cooking later in the day.

How to Sauté or brown in the Power Pressure Cooker XL

The Power Pressure Cooker doesn't come with a sauté button. Instead it recommends using the pressure cooking buttons without the lid on. Since the meat or chicken button has the longest cook time, it's a great choice for sautéing and browning. (However, it's been reported that new models now come with a sauté button!)

Releasing the Pressure

The symbols on the pressure valve are really easy to understand on the Power Pressure Cooker XL. Line up the image of the steam coming out with the triangle to hurriedly release the pressure – the open position. Line up the circle and the two triangles to pressure cook –the locked position.

The Power Pressure Cooker XL lid has an outer lid and an inner liner with a gasket. When you are cleaning the lid, make sure you remove and clean the liner – use the pull tab to separate the liner and gasket from the lid. Also remove the gasket from the liner and wash it.

When you're reattaching the liner and the gasket to the lid, make sure the pull tab is visible.

CHAPTER THREE

PRESSURE COOKER MUSHROOM MARSALA SOUP

Pressure Cooker Mushroom Marsala Soup is prepared with fresh ingredients for the finest flavor. Rosemary, thyme and a splash of dry Marsala wine improve the earthy elements of baby Portobello mushrooms. Relax and enjoy a cozy bowl tonight.

The good thing about making this soup in a pressure cooker is the fact that you're only using one pot and that makes clean up a quick one. The hand held immersion blender used to blend the cooked ingredients is also a big help. Instead of transferring hot soup to a blender or food processor, just blend in the same pot.

Each component layered into a bowl of this creamy, Pressure Cooker Mushroom Marsala Soup is meant to charm the palate. The key notes that give it a distinctive savory warmth are the dry Marsala wine and fresh rosemary.

Ingredients:

- 2 tablespoons butter

- 1 cup onion, diced

- 1 teaspoon salt

- 1 pound baby Portobello mushrooms, chopped

- 2 garlic cloves, chopped

- 1/2 cup dry Marsala wine

- 1/8 teaspoon freshly ground black pepper

- 2 teaspoons fresh rosemary, finely chopped

- 2 teaspoons fresh thyme, finely chopped

- 4 cups chicken stock

- 2 tablespoons butter

- 2 tablespoons flour

- 2 cups heavy whipping cream

- Freshly grated Parmesan and chopped parsley for garnish

How to prepare

- Preheat the pressure cooker. Melt 2 tablespoons butter. Add in the onion and one teaspoon of salt. Sauté it for two minutes.

- Add in the mushrooms, garlic and pepper. Sauté them until the mushrooms begin to discharge their moisture. Add in Marsala wine and sauté 2 minutes. Add in chicken stock, rosemary, and thyme.

- Position the lid on and turn to locked position. Turn the steam release valve to sealing. Select high pressure and 3 minutes cook time.

- While the mixture is cooking, melt 2 tablespoons butter in a sauté pan over medium-high heat. Whisk in 2 tablespoons of flour a little at a time until even. Cook for one minute, remove from heat and set aside.

- When the timer beeps, use a quick pressure release. Take off the lid, press the sauté button and allow the mixture to come to a boil. Mix in the butter and flour mixture and boil for 2 minutes. Turn off pressure cooker, and use an immersion blender to blend the mixture till smooth.

- Stir in the cream and ladle the soup into serving bowls.

- Garnish with fresh slices of Portobello mushrooms, freshly grated Parmesan and chopped parsley.

- Set a couple of the mushrooms aside and slice for garnishing the finished soup.

CHAPTER FOUR

PRESSURE COOKER CRANBERRY BAKED FRENCH TOAST

This luscious Pressure Cooker Cranberry Baked French Toast is the ideal holiday breakfast. Tart fresh cranberries in a sweet orange sauce are topped with cubed Challah bread soaked in butter, milk, and eggs, and then "baked" to make a bread pudding style French toast.

Ingredients:

Cranberry Orange Sauce

- 2 cups fresh cranberries, washed
- 1/4 cup fresh orange juice
- 1/2 cup granulated sugar
- 1/4 teaspoon ground cinnamon
- 1/4 teaspoon salt

French toast

- 4 tablespoons butter, melted
- 1/2 cup sugar
- 2 cups whole milk

- 3 eggs, beaten

- Finely grated zest from 1 orange

- 1 teaspoon vanilla extract

- 1/4 teaspoon salt

- 1 loaf Challah bread, cubed

How to prepare

- Bring cranberries, orange juice, 1/2 cup sugar, 1/4 teaspoon cinnamon, and 1/4 teaspoon salt to a boil in a saucepan over medium-high heat. Cook until the berries have popped and thickened slightly for about 5 minutes. Take out from heat. Pour into a buttered 7×3" cake pan, or similar glass or metal baking dish. (Make sure it fits in your pressure cooking pot.)

- In a big bowl, whisk together melted butter and 1/2 cup sugar. Add in milk, beaten eggs, orange zest, vanilla, and salt. Mix in cubed bread. Let rest until the bread soak up the milk, stirring infrequently.

- Spread bread mixture on top of cranberry sauce in pan. Prepare a foil sling for lifting the dish out of the pressure cooking pot by taking an 18" strip of foil and folding it lengthwise twice.

- Pour in 1 cup water into the pressure cooking pot and position the trivet in the bottom. Center the pan on the foil strip and place it into the pressure cooker.

- Lock the lid in place. Pick High Pressure and set the timer for 25 minutes. When beep sounds, turn off pressure cooker, and do a quick pressure release to release the pressure. When valve drops carefully remove lid.

- Take off dish from pressure cooking pot. If you want, place dish under the broiler to brown up the top.

CHAPTER FIVE

TASTY CRANBERRY APPLE SAUCE

This sauce is naturally sweetened, fast and easy. This Pressure Cooker Cranberry Apple Sauce will play a big role at any holiday meal.

With the combination of orange juice, apple cider, maple syrup, and a honey crisp apple, this cranberry sauce is an ideal balance of tart and sweet and is heavenly on turkey.

Ingredients:

- 12 oz fresh or frozen cranberries, rinsed

- zest and juice of 1 large orange

- 1 honey crisp apple, peeled and chopped

- ½ cup apple cider

- ½ cup pure maple syrup

How to prepare

- Pour all of the ingredients into the pressure cooker pot and stir well. Secure the lid and turn pressure release knob to a sealed position. Cook at high pressure for 5 minutes.

- When cooking is finished, use a natural release for 5 minutes and then release any remaining pressure. If liquid sprays while releasing the pressure, quickly turn the valve to the sealed position and wait for 5 more minutes.

- Simmer for 2-3 minutes to thicken. Sauce will thicken further as it cools. Serve warm or can also be made up to a week in advance and stored in the fridge. Freeze very well.

CHAPTER SIX

JAPANESE PRESSURE COOKER BEEF CURRY

This is a must try Japanese Pressure Cooker Beef Curry Recipe! Recreate one of Tokyo's most highly rated Japanese Curry Beef Stew using simple everyday ingredients. Eat this and live with no regrets.

Ingredients

- 2 pounds (937g) USDA Choice Grade Chuck Steak (Canada AAA Grade blade steak), 1.5 inch in thickness

- 6 medium garlic cloves, chopped

- ¾ cup (190ml) unsalted chicken stock

- 2 – 3 (74g – 110g) Japanese curry roux cube or homemade Japanese curry roux

- 1 tablespoon (15ml) Japanese soy sauce

Caramelized Onion Purée

- 1.5 pound (680g) yellow onions and shallots, thinly sliced

- 3 tablespoon (45g) unsalted butter

- ⅓ teaspoon (1.3g) baking soda

- Kosher salt and ground black pepper to taste

How to prepare

- Heat up your pressure cooker (Instant Pot: press Sauté button) over medium heat. Ensure your pot is as hot as it can be (Instant Pot: wait until indicator says HOT).

- Melt 3 tbsp (45g) unsalted butter in pressure cooker. Add in sliced onions, shallots, ⅓ tsp (1.3g) baking soda. Sauté until moisture starts to come out of the onions (~5 minutes). Close lid and pressure cook at High Pressure for 20 minutes, then Quick Release. Open lid.

- Reduce until Caramelized (takes roughly 16 – 17 minutes) there will be lots of moisture from the onions. Reduce until most moisture has evaporated over medium high heat (Instant Pot: press cancel, Sauté button and Adjust once to Sauté More function). Stir constantly with a silicone spatula.

- Once most moisture has evaporated, adjust to medium heat (Instant Pot: press cancel and Sauté). Stir until onions are deep golden brown and all moisture has evaporated. Season with kosher salt and ground black pepper to taste. Remove caramelized onion purée and set aside.

- Brown the Chuck Steak. Adjust to medium high heat (Instant Pot: press cancel, Sauté button and Adjust once to Sauté More function. Wait until indicator says HOT).

- Lightly season chuck steak with kosher salt & black pepper. Add 1 tbsp (15ml) of olive oil in the pot. Ensure to coat oil over whole bottom of the pot.

- Add seasoned chuck roast in the pot. Brown it for 6 – 8 minutes on each side without flipping. Remove and set aside on a chopping board.

- Sauté the Garlic. Add in chopped garlic and stir until fragrant (about 30secs).

- Deglaze. Pour in roughly ½ cup (100 ml) of unsalted chicken stock and completely deglaze the pot by scrubbing all flavorful brown bits with a wooden spoon.

- Pressure Cook the Chuck Roast. Cut chuck steak into 1.5 – 2 inches stew cubes, and place them along with its meat juice back to the pot. Add remaining unsalted chicken stock, 1 tbsp (15ml) Japanese soy sauce and caramelized onion purée. Mix well. Close lid and pressure cook at High Pressure for 32 minutes + 10 minutes Natural Release. Turn off heat. Release remaining pressure. Open lid.

- Make the Japanese Curry. Taste the caramelized onion beef stew. Mix in the Japanese curry roux cubes one by one while tasting for the right balance of flavors. Taste and add more curry roux or

Japanese soy sauce if necessary. We used roughly 2.5 (95g) Japanese curry roux.

- Serve over Calrose rice. Sprinkled some mozzarella cheese on top and baked it in the oven until the cheese melted and browned.

CHAPTER SEVEN

BABY BACK RIBS

Ingredients

- 2 racks baby back ribs

- 4 tbsp. granulated garlic powder

- 2 tbsp. onion powder

- 1 tbsp. cumin

- 1 tbsp. coriander

- 2 cups smoky barbecue sauce

How to prepare

- In a little bowl, thoroughly blend together the dry ingredients.

- Cut the racks into two so that they can easily fit in the Power Cooker. Season them uniformly with the seasoning blend.

- Place 1 cup of water in the Power Cooker, then add the ribs, side by side. Evenly pour the BBQ sauce over the ribs. Select cook mode then set cook time to 25 minutes.

Optional:

- Have your broiler preheated to high. Place the ribs in a single layer on a tin foil lined baking sheet and broil the ribs on each side until browned well, about 3-5 minutes per side.

- Brush the ribs with the barbecue sauce from the pot and serve.

CHAPTER EIGHT

RED BEANS AND RICE

Ingredients

- 1 lb. dried red beans
- 5 slices bacon, chopped
- 1 ham hock, smoked
- 2 cloves garlic, peeled and minced
- 2 tbsp. olive oil
- 1 large onion, peeled and diced
- 1 medium red bell pepper, seeded and diced
- ¾ cup tomato purée
- 2 tbsp. cilantro, chopped
- 4 cups chicken stock
- 3 cups rice, cooked

How to prepare:

- Put the bacon in the inner pot and set the Power Cooker on brown mode. Once the bacon is cooked add the onion and garlic and cook for 5 minutes.

- Add in the remaining ingredients, except cooked rice. Set the machine to stew mode. (Default time 30 minutes and default pressure 70).

- Serve over cooked rice.

CHAPTER NINE

MINI RIGATONESE BOLOGNESE

Ingredients

- 2 tbsp. olive oil

- 1 lb. ground beef

- 1 lb. ground pork

- 1 medium onion, peeled and finely chopped

- 2 cloves garlic, peeled and minced

- 1 medium carrot, peeled and finely chopped

- 3/4 cup dry, red wine

- 3 tbsp. tomato paste

- 2 cups crushed canned tomatoes

- 3/4 cup beef broth

- pinch cayenne pepper

- 6 tbsp. finely grated Parmigiano-Reggiano

- 1 lb. mini rigatoni pasta, cooked to preference

- salt & pepper to taste

How to prepare

- Place the oil in the inner pot and set the Power Cooker on brown mode. Place the pork and beef in the pot and cook for 10 minutes.

- Add the onion, garlic, and carrot and cook for 5 minutes.

- Add the remaining ingredients expect for the pasta and the cheese. Set the pressure adjust mode to 50. Set the cook time to 20 minutes.

- Serve over pasta with Parmigiano-Reggiano cheese.

CHAPTER TEN

PRESSURE COOKER STUFFED GREEN PEPPER CASSEROLE

This (Instant Pot) Pressure Cooker Stuffed Green Pepper Casserole comes with all the flavors of stuffed green peppers in an easy-to-make casserole. If you like stuffed green peppers, you're absolutely going to love this Insta Pot casserole.

Ingredients:

- 1 lb. lean ground beef

- 1/2 cup chopped onion

- 2 cloves garlic, minced

- 2 large green peppers, chopped

- handful of spinach leaves, coarsely chopped

- 1 (14.5 oz) can diced tomatoes with juices

- 1 (8 oz) can tomato sauce

- 1/2 cup beef broth

- 1/2 cup long grain rice (uncooked)

- 1 tablespoon Worcestershire sauce

- 1/2 teaspoon salt

- 1/4 teaspoon pepper

- 1 cup shredded mozzarella cheese

How to prepare

- Preheat the pressure cooking pot on the Browning/Sauté setting. Add in the ground beef and onion and cook until the beef is browned and crumbled. Add in garlic and sauté 1 minute more.

- Stir in green peppers, spinach, tomatoes, tomato sauce, beef broth, rice, Worcestershire sauce, salt, and pepper. Lock lid in place, select High Pressure and 4 minutes cook time. When timer beeps, do a natural release for 10 minutes, then release any remaining pressure with a quick pressure release.

- Turn off pressure cooker and pour casserole into an oven-safe baking dish. Sprinkle the cheese on top of casserole and broil until the cheese is melted and starting to brown.

CHAPTER ELEVEN

PRESSURE COOKER GREEN CHILE PORK CARNITAS

Moist, flavor-packed, and fall apart in your mouth tender, these Pressure Cooker Green Chile Pork Carnitas are the ideal solution for a quick family friendly dinner!

Ingredients:

- 2-3 lbs pork shoulder, cut into 6-8 pieces

- 2 tablespoons olive oil

- 1 teaspoon salt

- 1/2 teaspoon black pepper

- 1 large jalapeño, seeded and stem removed

- 1 green bell pepper, seeded and stem removed

- 1 poblano pepper, seeded and stem removed

- 1 lb tomatillos, husks removed and quartered

- 3 cloves garlic, peeled

- 1 onion, quartered

- 1 teaspoon cumin

- 1 teaspoon oregano

- 2 cups chicken broth

- 2 bay leaves

Toppings

- Tortillas (I prefer a flour/corn hybrid)

- Queso Fresco

- Red onion, diced

- Cilantro, roughly chopped

How to prepare

- Rub pork shoulder pieces with salt and pepper then place in pressure cooker and brown in olive oil for 2-3 minutes.

- Add in jalapeño, green pepper, poblano, quartered tomatillos, garlic, onion, cumin, oregano, chicken broth, and bay leaves.

- Give a swift stir and lock lid, then set it to high pressure for 55 minutes.

- Do a natural release and then release remaining pressure with a fast release after 10 minutes.

- Take out the meat from pressure cooker and add broth with peppers to blender and puree.

- Shred meat with fork and then add it back to pressure cooker along with green chile sauce.

- Stir to mix and then serve in tortillas topped with crumbled queso fresco, red onion, and cilantro.

CHAPTER TWELVE

PRESSURE COOKER CRUSTLESS TOMATO SPINACH QUICHE

The quiche is also filled up with diced vine ripened tomatoes and green onions, then topped up with thinly sliced tomatoes and Parmesan cheese. It's a simple to make meal that made plenty for dinner, and breakfast the next day

Ingredients:

- 12 large eggs

- 1/2 cup milk

- 1/2 teaspoon salt

- 1/4 teaspoon fresh ground black pepper

- 3 cups fresh baby spinach, roughly chopped

- 1 cup diced seeded tomato

- 3 large green onions, sliced

- 4 tomato slices for topping the quiche

- 1/4 cup shredded Parmesan cheese

How to prepare

- Put in a trivet in the bottom of the pressure cooker pot and add 1 1/2 cups water.

- In a big bowl whisk together the eggs, milk, salt and pepper. Add in spinach, tomato, and green onions to a 1 1/2 quart baking dish and mix well. Pour egg mixture over the veggies and stir to combine. Carefully place sliced tomatoes on top and sprinkle with Parmesan cheese.

- Use a sling to position the dish on the trivet in the pressure cooking pot. Lock lid in place. Select High Pressure and 20 minutes cook time. When timer beeps, turn off, wait 10 minutes, then use a quick pressure release.

- Gently open the lid, lift out the dish and if you want, broil until lightly browned.

CHAPTER THIRTEEN

CHOCOLATE POT DE CREME

This Pressure Cooker Chocolate Pots de Crème is quick and easy to make. They're rich, creamy and decadently delicious.

Ingredients:

- 1 1/2 cups heavy cream

- 1/2 cup whole milk

- 5 large egg yolks

- 1/4 cup sugar

- pinch of salt

- 8 ounces bittersweet chocolate, melted

- whipped cream and grated chocolate for decoration, optional

How to prepare

- In a small saucepan, bring the cream and milk to a simmer.

- In a large mixing bowl, whisk simultaneously egg yolks, sugar, and salt. Slowly whisk in the hot cream and milk. Whisk in chocolate until evenly combined Pour into 6 custard cups. (I used 1/2 pint mason jars.)

- Add in 1 1/2 cups of water to the pressure cooker and position the trivet in the bottom. Place 3 cups on the trivet and place a second trivet on top of the cups. Stack the remaining three cups on top of the second trivet.

- Lock the lid in place. Select High Pressure and set the timer for 6 minutes. When beep sounds, turn off pressure cooker and use a natural pressure release for 15 minutes and then do a fast pressure release to release any residual pressure. When valve drops carefully remove lid.

- Gently remove the cups to a wire rack to cool uncovered. When cool, refrigerate covered with plastic wrap for at least 4 hours or overnight.

CHAPTER FOURTEEN

PRESSURE COOKER SMOKY HAM HOCK AND PINTO BEAN SOUP

This comforting bowl of Pressure Cooker Smoky Ham Hock and Pinto Bean Soup is loaded with textures and flavors. You'll like the soft and moist ham lending its' smoky flavors to the fulfilling soup.

Ingredients

- Smoked ham hock
- Small onion
- Garlic cloves
- Cumin powder
- Dried oregano
- Ground black pepper
- Bay leaves
- Pinto beans
- Homemade unsalted chicken stock
- Season: Kosher salt to taste
- Garnish: cilantro & minced tomatoes

How to prepare

- You can prepare this delicious dish using 2 different cooking methods for this recipe

- Dump-and-Go Version: This is an easy no fuss method where you put all the ingredients into the pressure cooker, then set-it-and-forget-it. Season, garnish, and then serve!

- More Texture & Flavors Version: Split the beans into 2 sets and place them into the pressure cooker at 2 different times. This version results in an overall flavorful dish full of texture.

CHAPTER FIFTEEN

PRESSURE COOKER KOREAN CHICKEN THIGHS

Delight your taste buds with the umami sweet and spicy flavors in this Pressure Cooker Korean Chicken Thighs recipe. Its fast and simple enough for a weeknight, and classy enough to steal the show at your next dinner party!

Ingredients:

Korean BBQ Sauce

- 1/2 cup gochujang

- 1/4 cup hoisin sauce

- 1/4 cup ketchup

- 1/4 cup mirin

- 1/4 cup soy sauce (I like tamari)

- 1/4 cup sake rice wine

- 1 tablespoon unseasoned rice vinegar

- 1 tablespoon fresh ginger, grated or minced

- 1/2 tablespoon garlic, minced

The Chicken

- 2 tablespoons vegetable oil

- 2 pounds bone-in chicken thighs, skin removed

- 1 medium onion, chopped

- 1 tablespoon ginger, minced or grated

- 1 teaspoon garlic, minced

- 1 cup chicken broth

- 2 teaspoons cornstarch

- 1/4 cup broth or water

How to prepare

Korean BBQ Sauce

- Whisk the ingredients (gochujang through together in a medium bowl. Remove and set aside 1 cup for finishing the sauce.

The Chicken

- Using the pressure cooker or a pan on the stove, brown the chicken pieces on both sides in the vegetable oil. Set it aside.

- Add the onion, ginger, and garlic. Cook until the onion is soft. Add the chicken pieces and onion mixture to the pressure cooker.

- Mix the chicken broth with the Korean BBQ sauce remaining in the prep bowl (after removing 1 cup). Add to the pressure cooker with the chicken.

- Lock the lid, and cook on high pressure for 15 minutes. Release the pressure.

- Take out 1 cup of cooking liquid to a medium sauce pan. Mix the cornstarch with broth or water. Bring the cooking liquid to a boil, and add the cornstarch slurry a bit at a time until thickened as desired. Add in the reserved BBQ sauce. Stir until combined and bubbly.

To Serve

With the use of a slotted spoon, remove chicken pieces to a platter. Pour the sauce over the top, and garnish with slice scallions. Serve with jasmine rice.

CHAPTER SIXTEEN

PRESSURE COOKER VEGETABLE BEEF AND RICE SOUP

This Pressure Cooker Vegetable Beef and Rice Soup is a tasty, hearty meal that comes together fast and is on the table in a flash.

Ingredients:

- 1lb. lean ground beef

- 1 tablespoon oil

- 1 large onion, diced

- 1 rib celery, chopped

- 3 cloves garlic, finely chopped or pressed

- 2 14-ounce cans beef broth

- 1 14-ounce can crushed tomatoes

- 1 12-ounce bottle Original or Spicy Hot V8 juice

- 1/2 cup long grain white rice

- 1 15-ounce can garbanzo beans, drained and rinsed

- 1 large potato, peeled and diced into 1-inch pieces

- 2 carrots, peeled then sliced into thin coins

- 1/2 cup frozen peas, thawed

- salt and pepper

How to prepare

- Preheat the pressure cooking pot using the browning or sauté setting. Add in ground beef to the pressure cooking pot and cook it until browned. Remove to a plate lined with paper towels.

- Add in oil to the pressure cooking pot. Add in onion and celery and cook, stirring intermittently until the onion is soft, about 5 minutes. Add in garlic and cook 1 minute more.

- Add in beef broth, tomatoes, V8 juice, rice, garbanzo beans, potatoes, carrots, and browned ground beef to the pot and stir to mix. Lock lid in place, select High Pressure and 4 minutes cook time. When timer beeps, turn off pressure cooker and do a quick pressure release.

- Stir in peas and season with salt and pepper to taste.

CHAPTER SEVENTEEN

PRESSURE COOKER ORANGE CHICKEN

Pressure cooker orange chicken is one of the easiest and finest pressure cooker chicken recipes to make when you want an Asian meal at home. Soft bite-size pieces of chicken, in a sweet, spicy, orange sauce. This tasty Pressure Cooker Orange Chicken can be on the table in about 20 minutes.

Ingredients:

- 4 large boneless skinless chicken breasts, diced (about 2 lbs.)

- 1/4 cup soy sauce

- 1/4 cup water + 3 tablespoons water, divided

- 2 tablespoons brown sugar

- 1 tablespoon rice wine vinegar

- 1 teaspoon sesame oil

- 1/4 teaspoon chili garlic sauce

- 1/2 cup orange marmalade

- 3 tablespoons cornstarch

- 2 green onions, chopped, optional

- red pepper flakes, optional

How to prepare

- Add in chicken, soy sauce, 1/4 cup water, brown sugar, rice wine vinegar, sesame oil, and chili garlic sauce to the pressure cooking pot and stir to mix. Pressure cook on high pressure for 3 minutes. When timer beeps, turn pressure cooker off and do a quick pressure release. Add in marmalade to the pot and stir to combine.

- In a small bowl, dissolve cornstarch in 3 tablespoons water and add to the pot. Select Sauté and simmer until sauce is thick and syrupy.

- Serve it topped with green onions and red pepper flakes if you want.

Note:

- You can cook rice while you are cooking the chicken. Here's how to do it; Use a 7×3 inch round cake pan or similar dish, and add in rice ingredients. Put a rack on top of the chicken in the pressure cooking pot, and place the cake pan on top of the rack.

POWER PRESSURE COOKER XL COOKBOOK

CHAPTER EIGHTEEN

PRESSURE COOKER PULLED PORK

Make this irresistible Pressure Cooker Pulled Pork Recipe with your own Dry Rub and BBQ Sauce. Tender, juicy pulled pork exploding with sweet & smoky flavors. Making BBQ Pulled Pork has never been this quick and easy! You have to try it.

Ingredients

- 4 pounds (~1.8 kg) pork shoulder picnic (Cut into 4 – 8 pieces)

- 1 tablespoons (15 ml) olive oil

Pulled Pork Dry Rub:

- 2 tablespoons (25 g) brown sugar

- 2 teaspoons (5 g) chili powder

- 2 teaspoons (4 g) black pepper

- 1 teaspoon (2.4 g) onion powder

- 1 teaspoon (2.8 g) garlic powder

- 1 teaspoon (2.3 g) cinnamon powder

- 1 teaspoon (3 g) kosher salt

- ½ teaspoon (1 g) cumin seed, ground

- ½ teaspoon (1 g) fennel seed, ground

- ¼ teaspoon (0.5 g) cayenne pepper

BBQ Sauce for Pulled Pork:

- 1 medium onion, minced

- 3 garlic cloves, minced

- 1 cup (250 ml) ketchup

- ½ cup (125 ml) water

- ⅛ cup (31ml) maple syrup

- ⅛ cup (31ml) honey

- 2 tablespoons (30 ml) apple cider vinegar

- 2 tablespoons (30 ml) Dijon mustard

- 1 tablespoon (25 g) brown sugar

How to prepare

- Rub the Pulled Pork Dry Rub: Combine all the dry rub ingredients and rub it all over the pork shoulder picnic pieces. Then, put the pork shoulder picnic in the fridge for 30 minutes to overnight.

- Heat up the Pressure Cooker: Heat up your pressure cooker (Instant Pot: press Sauté button). Be sure your pot is as hot as it can be when you place the pork shoulder meat into the pot (For Instant Pot: wait until the indicator says HOT).

- Optional Step - Brown the Pork Shoulder: Add in 1 tablespoon (15 ml) of olive oil into the pot. Make sure you coat the oil over the whole bottom of the pot. Put the pork shoulder pieces into the pot. Brown the pork shoulder on all sides. Remove and set aside.

- Add the BBQ Sauce and Deglaze: Pour in half of the Pulled Pork BBQ Sauce and deglaze the base of the pot. Then, put in the remaining BBQ sauce blend.

- Pressure Cook the Pork Shoulder (See Tips): Place all the pork shoulder pieces into the pot. If you left the skin on make sure the skin side is facing up. Close lid and pressure cook at High Pressure for 60 minutes (see notes). Turn off the heat and fully Natural Release (roughly 15 minutes).

- Fork Tender Check: Open the lid carefully. Take one piece of pork shoulder out and see if you can shred through the meat easily with two forks. If it is not fork-tender, cook for an additional 10 to 20 minutes at High Pressure, fully Natural Release.

- Shred the Pork & De-Fat the Sauce: Use some cool Pulled Pork Shredder Claws or two regular forks to shred the pork shoulder meat. Use a fat separator to separate the fat from the BBQ sauce.

- Season, Reduce, Serve: Reduce the BBQ sauce to your desired thickness. Taste the BBQ sauce and add in additional brown sugar or kosher salt if desired. Place the pulled pork back into the BBQ sauce. Mix well and serve!

CHAPTER NINETEEN

LOADED INSTANT POT MAC AND CHEESE

Prepare this Loaded Instant Pot Mac and Cheese Recipe right now. Piping hot elbow macaroni swimming in creamy cheddar cheese sauce. Sprinkled with buttery toasted golden breadcrumbs, smoky crispy bacon bits, and crunchy scallions. Indulge in this kid-friendly comfort food.

Ingredients

- 16 ounces (454 g) elbow macaroni

- 4 cups (1 L) cold running water

- 4 tablespoons (60 g) unsalted butter

- 14 ounces (397 g) sharp cheddar, freshly grated

- 6 ounces (170 g) mild cheddar or American cheese, freshly grated

- Kosher salt and ground black pepper

Wet Ingredients

- 2 large eggs, beaten

- 12 ounces (355 ml) can evaporated milk

- 1 teaspoon (5 ml) Sriracha sauce or Frank's hot sauce

- 1 teaspoon (2 g) ground mustard

Bacon Bits & Scallion

- 4 – 8 strips bacon

- 2 stalks scallion, finely chopped

Buttery Crispy Breadcrumbs

- ½ cup (31 g) panko breadcrumbs

- 1 tablespoon (15 ml) olive oil

- 1 tablespoon (15 g) unsalted butter

- Kosher salt to taste

How to prepare

- Crispy Bacon Bits: Position bacon on a baking sheet lined with parchment paper. Put it on the middle rack of a preheated 400°F oven. Bake bacon until it is crispy and golden-brown. Set a timer for roughly 18 - 20 minutes. Place them on a paper towel to soak up the excess fat. Cut into bacon bits.

- Pressure Cook the Elbow Macaroni: Add 16 ounces (454 g) of elbow macaroni, 4 cups (1 L) of water, and in a pinch of kosher salt into your pressure cooker. Close the lid and pressure cook at High Pressure for 4 minutes. Do a steady quick release. There is a slight chance that a small amount of foam will come out with the steam. Have a towel around just in case. Open lid cautiously.

- Prepare the Crispy Breadcrumbs: While the macaroni is pressure cooking, heat a skillet over medium heat. Add in 1 tablespoon (15 g) of unsalted butter, 1 tablespoon (15 ml) of olive oil, and ½ cup (31 g) of panko breadcrumbs to the skillet. Toast the breadcrumbs until it is golden brown. Taste and add kosher salt for seasoning.

- Mix Wet Ingredients: In a medium mixing bowl, beat 2 large eggs and mix in 1 tsp (2 g) ground mustard, 1 tsp (5 ml) Sriracha, and 12 ounces (355 ml) evaporated milk. Mix it well.

- Make the Mac & Cheese: Keep heat on low or medium low (Instant Pot: use the keep warm function). Give it a fast stir and check to see if there is excessive liquid in the pot. Drain if necessary. Place 4 tablespoons (60 g) of unsalted butter into the pressure cooked macaroni. Mix well with a silicone spatula and let the butter melt.

- Pour in the wet ingredients and mix well. Add in the grated cheese ⅓ portion at a time and stir frequently until the cheese fully melts.

- If the mac and cheese is too runny, turn the heat to medium (Instant Pot: Use Sauté Less function - Click cancel, Sauté and Adjust button twice) to reduce it down.

- Taste & Season: Taste and season with kosher salt and ground black pepper. You will most likely need quite a few pinches of kosher salt to brighten the dish.

- Serve: Generously sprinkle crispy breadcrumb, bacon bits, then scallion over a bowl of macaroni & cheese and serve immediately!

CHAPTER TWENTY

NEW YORK INSTANT POT CHEESE CAKE

Make this Easy New York Instant Pot Cheesecake Recipe. Pamper yourself or impress your guests with your choice of Smooth & Creamy or Rich & Dense Pressure Cooker Cheesecake with a crisp crust.

Ingredients

Crust

- 10 (120g) graham crackers, finely ground

- 3 - 4 tablespoons (42g - 56g) unsalted butter, melted

- Pinch of sea salt

- 2 teaspoons - 1½ tablespoon (8.3g - 19g) brown sugar (depends on desired sweetness)

- Optional: ¼ cup (32g) all-purpose flour (for blind-baking crust)

Cheesecake Batter (7 inches x 3 inches)

- 16 ounces (454g) Philadelphia cream cheese, room temperature

- 2 large eggs, room temperature

- ⅔ cup (133g) white sugar

- ½ cup (120g) sour cream, room temperature

- 2 tablespoons (16g) cornstarch

- 2 teaspoons (10ml) vanilla extract

- 2 pinches of sea salt

How to prepare

Critical Tips before You Start

- We recommend using a Hand Mixer to mix the cheesecake batter instead of a Stand Mixer. Stand Mixers are usually more powerful, so you can easily over-mix and introduce too much air into the cheesecake batter. This may result in a puffy soufflé-style cheesecake.

Preparation

- Put 16 ounces (454g) cream cheese, 2 large eggs, ½ cup (120g) sour cream on counter-top to reach room temperature. Then, melt the 3 - 4 tablespoons (42g - 56g) unsalted butter.

- **Tip:** this is grave for your cheesecake's success, so please make sure all the above ingredients are at room temperature before you begin. If not, you may end up with lumpy fluff top cheesecake. So don't skip this step!

PART A: **Prepare the crust**

- Ground Graham Crackers: Smoothly ground 120g graham crackers in a food processor. Or put the graham crackers in a Ziploc bag and roll them with a rolling pin.

- Mix Crust Mixture: In a small mixing bowl, mix up finely ground graham crackers, a pinch of sea salt, 2 tsp - 1½ tbsp (8.3g - 19g) brown sugar together with a fork.

- Perfectionist's Step - Add Flour (if blind-baking for firmer & crisper crust): mix in ¼ cup (32g) all-purpose flour.

- Add Melted Unsalted Butter: Mix in roughly 3 - 4 tbsp (42g - 56g) unsalted butter till the mixture sticks together.

- Line Pan: Line the side and bottom of cheesecake pan with a parchment paper.

- Form Crust: Pour in the graham cracker crumbs mixture. Carefully press down the crumbs with a ramekin or Mason jar to form an even layer. You can also use a spoon for the edges.

Firm Crust

- Method 1 - Freeze: Place cheesecake pan in freezer while you make the cheesecake batter.

- Method 2 - Blind-Bake (for firmer & crisper crust): Place crust in a 325°F oven for 15 minutes.

PART B: Make dense cheesecake batter

- Mix Sugar Mixture: Mix 2 tbsp (16g) cornstarch, 2 pinches of sea salt, and ⅔ cup (133g) white sugar together in a small mixing bowl.

- Briefly Beat Cream Cheese: In a medium mixing bowl, briefly break up the 454g cream cheese by beating it for 10 seconds with a hand mixer using low speed.

- Mix in Sugar Mixture: Add in half the sugar mixture and beat until just incorporated using low speed (roughly 20 - 30 seconds). Scrape down the sides and hand mixer with a silicone spatula every time a new ingredient is added. Add in the remaining sugar mixture and beat until just incorporated using low speed (roughly 20 - 30 seconds).

- Add Sour Cream & Vanilla Extract: Add ½ cup (120g) sour cream and 2 tsp (10 ml) vanilla extract to the cream cheese mixture. Beat until just incorporated using low speed (20 - 30 seconds).

- Blend in Eggs: Mix in the two eggs using low speed, one at a time. Mix until just incorporated (about 15 – 20 seconds with a hand mixer & less time if you are using a powerful stand mixer). Try not to over-mix on this step. Scrape down the sides and hand mixer with a silicone spatula and fold a few times to make sure everything is fully included.

- Pour Batter in Pan: Pour cream cheese batter in cheesecake pan.

- Remove Air Bubbles for Smooth Surface: Tap cheesecake pan against the counter to let air bubbles rise to the surface. Burst the air bubbles with a toothpick or fork.

- Tap until you are content. Make sure the surface is clear of air bubbles or fork marks.

PART C: Pressure cook cheesecake

- Method 1: Pour 1 cup (250 ml) of cold water in pressure cooker. Position cheesecake pan on top of a steamer rack (so, that it's not touching the water). Close lid and pressure cook at High Pressure for 26 minutes and Full Natural Release. Natural release will take approximately 7 minutes. Open lid slowly. Soak any condensation on surface by lightly tapping it with a soft paper towel.

- Perfectionist's Method 2 - Prevent Surface Dents: Put a steamer rack and pour 1 cup (250ml) of water in pressure cooker. Bring water to a boil (Instant Pot users: Press manual/Pressure Cook and set the time to 28 minutes).

- When the water begins to boil, place cheesecake pan on the steamer rack with a foil sling right away.

*Caution: Don't wait too long to place the cheesecake in pressure cooker, as it'll affect the cooking time. Place it right away once the water begins to boil. This prevents too much water from evaporating.

Immediately close the lid with Venting Knob at Venting Position. Turn Venting Knob to Sealing Position and let it pressure cook at High Pressure for 28 minutes and Full Natural Release. It should go up to pressure in roughly 1 minute. Natural release will take roughly 7 – 9 minutes. Open the lid gradually. Absorb any condensation on the surface by lightly tapping it with a soft paper towel.

PART D: Cool, chill, serves cheesecake

- Cool Cheesecake: Allow cheesecake to cool to room temperature with the lid open in the pressure cooker. Or place it on a wire rack to cool to room temperature.

- Release Cheesecake from Sidewall to Avoid Cracking: After cooling for 10 – 15 minutes, carefully run a thin paring knife between the sidewall and parchment paper to release the cheesecake from the pan. Pull the slightly wrinkled parchment paper lightly to straighten it out for a smooth side.

- Chill Cheesecake in Fridge: Once the cheesecake has completely cooled, place it in the refrigerator for at least 4 – 8 hours (preferably overnight).

- Serve: Remove cheesecake from the refrigerator. The best way to release the cheesecake from the bottom pan is warm the bottom of the pan to melt the butter. You can use a torch or heating pad for this step. Carefully peel off the parchment paper. Enjoy.

CHAPTER TWENTY ONE

PRESSURE COOKER BEEF STROGANOFF

Ingredients

- 2 pound beef, cut into 1 inch cubes

- 3 tablespoon olive oil

- 0.5 cup flour, for dredging beef

- 1 Medium onion, chopped

- 3 clove garlic, minced

- 3 cup Beef broth

- 2 tablespoon Tomato paste

- 1 tablespoon worchestershire sauce

- 2 cup Mushrooms, sliced

- 0.25 cup flour, for thickening sauce

- 0.5 teaspoon salt

- 0.5 teaspoon pepper

- 1 cup sour cream, for last step

How to prepare

Substituting with potato starch will make recipe Gluten Free.

- Put the inner pot into the Pressure Cooker. Put the oil in the inner pot. Press the Soup/Stew button.

- Cut beef round steak into 1-inch cubes, paint in 1/4 cup flour. In little batches, saute the beef in oil until browned on all sides. Add in the flour to make a roux.

- Sauté onion and garlic. Cook until it is translucent.

- Add in the remaining ingredients and stir.

- Place the lid on the Pressure Cooker and Lock. Switch the Pressure Release Valve to Close. Press the MEAT/CHICKEN button. Press the TIME ADJUSTMENT button and set to 20 minutes. Once the timer reaches 0, the Cooker will automatically switch to KEEP WARM. Press the cancel button.

- Switch the Pressure Release Valve to Open. When the steam is released totally, take away the lid. Stir potato flakes to thicken the sauce. Stir in gently and it will thicken in 2-3 minutes with the heat. If you want it thicker, add in more potato flakes. Stir in the sour cream. Serve over cooked egg noodles.

CHAPTER TWENTY TWO

TABOULI SALAD

Ingredients

- 1 cup bulgur wheat
- 1 cup water
- 0.75 cup minced parsley
- 0.5 cup minced cilantro
- 0.25 cup minced mint leaves
- 1 cup red onion chopped
- 3 plum tomatoes diced
- 0.5 cup Lemon juice
- 2 tablespoon olive oil
- 1 teaspoon salt
- 0.5 teaspoon pepper
- 1 Lemon, juiced
- 1 tablespoon diced scallions
- 0 teaspoon olive oil

- 1 pinch salt and freshly ground pepper to taste1/2

How to prepare

- Position the Inner Pot in the cooker. Press Beans lentil button, 5 minutes.

- Add in the bulgur wheat, water, salt and pepper

- Put the Lid on the cooker, lock Lid and switch the Pressure Valve to Closed.

- Once the timer reaches 0, the cooker will automatically switch to KEEP WARM. Press the CANCEL button. Natural release, when the steam is totally released, takes off the lid.

- Let the bulgur wheat cool.

- Mix the lemon juice and the olive oil together then pour over the bulgur wheat, and mix. Add in the parsley, mint, cilantro, onions, and tomatoes. Fold everything together.

- Transfer to a serving bowl garnish with lemon juice, scallions, and olive oil

CHAPTER TWENTY THREE

SWEET POTATO

Ingredients

- 5 sweet potatoes, peeled, diced large

- 1 cup water

- 1 pinch salt and freshly ground pepper to taste1/2

- 0.5 cup Heavy Cream

- 4 ounce butter

- 0.25 cup Brown Sugar

How to prepare

- Put the Inner Pot inside the cooker. Press Beans lentil button, 5 min

- Add in the sweet potatoes, water, salt and pepper

- Place the Lid on the cooker, lock Lid and switch the Pressure Valve to Closed.

- Once the timer reaches 0, the cooker will automatically switch to KEEP WARM. Press the CANCEL button. When the steam is completely released, remove the lid.

- With a wooden spoon, mash the potatoes until it is smooth; add in the cream, butter, and sugar.

- Ladle a portion out. Serve as side dish with your favorite Entrée.

CHAPTER TWENTY FOUR

THAI PEANUT NOODLE

These Thai Peanut Noodles are made with ingredients you probably already have in your kitchen! They're very easy to prepare, truly delicious, and take 10 minutes to whip up!

Ingredients

- 1 pound egg noodle, fettuccini nest

- 12 ounce Thai peanut sauce

- 2.5 cup water

- 8 ounce chicken, cooked strips

- 3 clove Garlic, sliced

- 1 Onion, sliced

- 1 tablespoon Grape seed oil

- 1 tablespoon scallions, green parts only sliced

- 2 ounce cilantro, chopped

- 0.5 lime, juiced

- 1 Salt and pepper to taste

How to prepare

- Put the Inner Pot in the pressure cooker. Put the Rice button. 6 min

- Add in the oil, sauté the onion and garlic for 1 min

- Now add in the chicken, water, peanut sauce, and stir. Then add in the noodles.

- Place the Lid on the cooker, lock Lid and switch the Pressure Valve to Closed.

- Once the timer reaches 0, the cooker will automatically switch to KEEP WARM. Press the CANCEL button. When the steam is completely released, remove the lid.

- Add in ½ the scallions and cilantro, stir. 7. Portion out each serving garnish with scallions, cilantro, lime juice and crushed peanuts.

CHAPTER TWENTY FIVE

PRESSURE COOKER SPAGHETTI SQUASH

Ingredients

- 1 spaghetti squash cut in half

- 1 cup water

- 2 tablespoon olive oil

- 1 teaspoon salt

- 0.5 teaspoon Freshly ground black pepper

How to prepare

- Position the Inner Pot in the cooker. Press Fish/Vegetable button for 2 minutes. Place the canning rack in the unit and the water.

- Place the spaghetti squash flesh side facing up. Drizzle oil over the flesh, then season with salt and pepper

- Put the Lid on the cooker, lock Lid and switch the Pressure Valve to Closed.

- Once the timer reaches 0, the cooker will automatically switch to KEEP WARM. Press the CANCEL button. Natural release, when the steam is totally released, take off the lid.

- When the squash is cool enough to handle pick them up with a towel. Now with a fork scrape out the flesh of the squash and it will fall stringy just like pasta. 6. Top or toss in your favorite sauce and Enjoy

CHAPTER TWENTY SIX

PICADILLO

Picadillo is one of the great dishes of the Cuban Diaspora: a soft, fragrant stew of ground beef and tomatoes, with raisins added for sweetness and olives for salt

Ingredients

- 1 pound ground beef

- 1 cup diced onions

- 1 cup diced green peppers

- 2 tablespoon garlic minced

- 1 tablespoon Garlic

- 2 tablespoon olive oil

- 0.5 cup olives, sliced, stuffed pimento

- 0.25 cup raisins

- 12 ounce tomato puree

- 0.25 cup Tomato paste

- 1 bay leaf

- 1 teaspoon cumin

How to prepare

- Position the Inner Pot in the cooker. Press Soup button, 10 minutes. Put the ground beef in the Inner Pot.

- Cook ground beef most of the way all through. Take out and drain excess fat.

- Begin with olive oil; add in the onions, green peppers and garlic. Sweat for few minutes.

- Add in the remaining ingredients stir. Place the Lid on the cooker, lock Lid and switch the Pressure Valve to Closed.

- Once the timer reaches 0, the cooker will automatically switch to KEEP WARM. Press the CANCEL button. When the steam is completely released, remove the lid.

- Ladle into a bowl over white rice. Serve with a side of fried plantains.

CHAPTER TWENTY SEVEN

PEACH AND CHERRY COMPOTE

This delicious summery dessert comes together in minutes.

Ingredients

- 10 peaches peeled and quartered

- 1 cup Cherries pitted

- 0.5 cup sugar

- 1 teaspoon Vanilla Extract

- 0.25 cup water

- 1 pinch salt

How to prepare

- Put the Inner Pot in the cooker. Pour in the peaches, cherries and the left over ingredients. Mix gently.

- Press Rice button. 6 minutes. Put the Lid on the cooker, lock Lid and switch the Pressure Valve to Closed.

- Once the timer reaches 0, the cooker will automatically switch to KEEP WARM. Press the CANCEL button. Natural release, when the steam is completely released, remove the lid.

- Ladle into a bowl.

- Pour over pound cake top with ice cream

CHAPTER TWENTY EIGHT

MEXICAN STREET CORN

You've had grilled corn on the cob before, but this is one step better. A common Mexican street food, it's absolutely delicious, and if you haven't yet experienced its awesomeness, try it today.

Ingredients

- 6 ears corn
- 1 cup water
- 1 cup sour cream
- 6 ounce cotija cheese
- 2 tablespoon Chili powder
- 3 tablespoon cilantro chopped
- 1 lime

How to prepare

- Place the Inner Pot in the cooker. Pour in the water. Place the Canning rack into the inner pot.
- Add in the corn
- Press Fish/Vegetable button. 2 minutes

- Place the Lid on the cooker, lock Lid and switch the Pressure Valve to Closed.

- Once the timer reaches 0, the cooker will automatically switch to KEEP WARM. Press the CANCEL button. When the steam is completely released, remove the lid.

- Remove from the inner pot. Wrap one end in parchment paper for easy handling

- Over a plate, garnish with chili powder, cheese, cilantro, and squeeze of lime.

CHAPTER TWENTY NINE

LENTIL SOUP

Recipe Type: Soups and Stews

Makes four Servings

Ingredients

- 2 cup Dry lentils

- 6 cup vegetable broth

- 1 Onion diced

- 2 carrots diced

- 2 celery stalks diced

- 2 tablespoon garlic minced

- 1 teaspoon cumin

- 2 Bay leaves

- 2 tablespoon olive oil

- 2 tablespoon chopped parsley and thyme

- 1 teaspoon salt

- 1 teaspoon fresh cracked black pepper

How to prepare

- Put the Inner Pot in the cooker. Put the Olive Oil in the Inner Pot. Press Rice/Risotto button. 6 minutes

- Put in the onions, carrots, and celery cook for 3 minutes, add in the garlic.

- Add in all the other ingredients. Position the Lid on the cooker, lock Lid and switch the Pressure Valve to Closed.

- Once the timer reaches 0, the cooker will automatically switch to KEEP WARM. Press the CANCEL button. Natural release, when the steam is totally released, take off the lid.

- Ladle into a bowl garnish with parsley and thyme

CHAPTER TWENTY NINE

INSTANT POT TERIYAKI CHICKEN AND RICE

Make this Easy Pressure Cooker Teriyaki Chicken and Rice Recipe and enjoy it. You'll love the sweet and savory teriyaki sauce soaked by the moist and tender chicken thighs over perfectly cooked Japanese rice. Your family will enjoy this delicious Japanese chicken teriyaki rice bowl!

Ingredients

- Chicken thighs (bone-in with skin)

- Teriyaki Sauce:

- Japanese soy sauce

- Mirin (Japanese rice cooking wine)

- Japanese cooking sake

- Sesame oil

- Sugar

- Rice: Water, Medium grain calrose rice

- Garlic cloves

- Ginger

- Cornstarch + water

Japanese style teriyaki sauce is a thickened sweet soy glaze called Tare Sauce (often used in grilling). It's actually very easy to make at home with a few simple ingredients. Generally, a basic teriyaki sauce is made of Japanese soy sauce, sugar, mirin (Japanese sweet cooking rice wine), and Japanese cooking sake.

*Ginger and garlic add aromatic flavors to the Teriyaki Sauce.

How to prepare

- Marinate the Chicken Thighs with Teriyaki Sauce: Mix together 4 tablespoons (60 ml) of Japanese soy sauce, 4 tablespoons (60 ml) of mirin, 4 tablespoons (60 ml) of sake, ¼ teaspoon (1.25 ml) of sesame oil, and 2 tablespoons (28 g) of sugar to make the teriyaki sauce mixture. Taste the blend to be sure it is balanced. Marinade the chicken thighs with the teriyaki sauce for 20 minutes.

- Vaporize Alcohol Content in Marinade: Put the marinade (without the chicken thighs) into the pressure cooker (Instant Pot: press Sauté button and click the adjust button to go to Sauté More function). Add 4 crushed garlic cloves and 1 very thin slice of ginger into the pressure cooker. Let the teriyaki sauce mixture come to a boil and let it boil for 30 seconds to let the alcohol in sake evaporate.

- Pressure Cook the Teriyaki Chicken and Rice: Add the chicken thighs into the pressure cooker with the skin side up. Position a steamer rack into the pressure cooker and carefully place a bowl with 1 cup of Calrose rice (230 g) onto the rack. Pour 1 cup of water (250 ml) into the bowl of rice. Be sure all the rice soaked with water. Immediately close the lid and cook at a High Pressure for 6 minutes. Turn off the heat and full Natural Release (roughly 10 minutes). Open the lid cautiously.

- (Optional Flavor Enhancing Step) Preheat Oven: While the teriyaki chicken and rice are cooking in the pressure cooker, preheat the oven to 450°F.

- Thicken the Teriyaki Sauce: Fluff the rice and set aside. Set the chicken thighs aside. Take out the ginger slice and garlic cloves. Turn heat to medium (Instant Pot: Press sauté button). Taste the seasoning one more time. Add in more Japanese soy sauce or sugar if want. Mix in the cornstarch with water and mix it into the teriyaki sauce one third at a time until the thickness you want.

- (Optional Flavor Enhancing Step) Apply Teriyaki Sauce and Finish in the Oven: Brush the teriyaki sauce all over the chicken thighs on both sides. Place the chicken thighs on a rack with the baking tray in the oven for 5 – 8 minutes.

- Serve: Serve immediately with rice and other side dishes.

CHAPTER THIRTY

BBQ INSTANT POT RIBS

Make this super simple no fuss 4 ingredients BBQ Instant Pot Ribs in just 40 minutes! Brushed with your favorite sweet and smoky BBQ sauce, these soft baby back ribs are finger licking' good. The ideal weeknight meal, last minute dinners, or cook them for your next BBQ.

Ingredients

- 1 rack baby back ribs

- ¼ cup your favorite BBQ sauce (We used Sweet Baby Ray's Barbecue Sauce)

- Kosher salt

- Ground black pepper

- Optional: a few drops of liquid smoke

How to prepare

- Prepare the Baby Back Ribs: Take out the membrane from the back of the ribs with a paper towel.

- Season the Baby Back Ribs: Season the Baby Back Ribs with rich amount of kosher salt and ground black pepper.

- Pressure Cook the Baby Back Ribs: Place 1 cup (250ml) of cold running tap water (or apple cider vinegar) and a trivet in the pressure cooker. Place the baby back ribs on top of the trivet. Close lid and pressure cook at High Pressure for 16 – 25 minutes. Adjust the timing according to your desire: 16 minutes (Tender with a bit of chew) to 25 minutes (fall off the bone). Turn off the heat and full Natural Release. Open the lid gently.

- Preheat Oven: While the baby back ribs are cooking in the pressure cooker, preheat the oven to 450F.

- Apply Sauce and Finish in the Oven: Rub your favorite BBQ sauce all over the baby back ribs on all sides including the bones. Put the baby back ribs with the baking tray in the oven for 10 – 15 minutes.

- Serve: Take out the ribs from the oven and serve!

CHAPTER THIRTY ONE

PRESSURE COOKER CHAR SIU (CHINESE BBQ PORK)

No need to take a trip to Chinatown! Prepare your own moist and super soft Instant Pot Char Siu Recipe (Pressure Cooker Char Siu Chinese BBQ Pork). Eat them fresh out of the oven. The bite full of sweet, delicious and savory flavors with slight melty texture will make your taste buds crave for more!

Ingredients

- 1 pound (454 g) pork butt meat, split the longer side in half

- 3 tablespoons (45 ml) honey

- 2 tablespoons (30 ml) light soy sauce (not low sodium soy sauce)

- 1 cup (250 ml) water

- A pinch Kosher salt to season

Marinade

- 1 tablespoon (15 ml) chu hou paste

- 2 cubes Chinese fermented red bean curd

- 3 tablespoons (45 ml) char siu sauce (Chinese BBQ sauce)

- ½ teaspoon (2.5 ml) sesame oil

- 2 tablespoons (30 ml) Shaoxing wine

- 1 teaspoon (2.8 g) garlic powder

- 1 tablespoon (15 ml) light soy sauce

How to prepare

- Marinate the pork: Use a fork to poke plenty holes all over the pork as deep as your fork can go. Marinate the pork for 30 minutes to 2 hours in a Ziploc bag with air squeezed out. Take out the pork and marinade from the bag. Pour 1 cup (250 ml) of water into the Ziploc bag and mix it with the left over marinade sticking onto the bag.

- Pressure cook the pork: Pour the marinade mixture into the pressure cooker then put the marinated pork butt meat in the pressure cooker on a steamer basket.

- Season the marinated pork with a pinch of kosher salt on both sides. Close lid and cook at a high pressure for 18 minutes, then 12 minutes natural release.

- Brush the pork: Mix 2 tablespoons (30 ml) of light soy sauce with honey in a small bowl. This sauce is to give some killer sweet taste and color to the outer layer of the pork butt meat. Brush this honey sauce richly onto the pork butt meat.

- Place pork in oven: Preheat oven to 450°F. Place pork in oven and cook for roughly 4 - 6 minutes per side until the honey sauce on both sides are browned with some black bits.

- Serve: Serve the char siu with rice or noodles and the leftover honey sauce on the side.

CHAPTER THIRTY TWO

PRESSURE COOKER PORK CHOPS IN HK TOMATO SAUCE

Make this simple Instant Pot Pork Chops in HK Tomato Sauce Recipe. Soft and moist pork chops, immersed in delicious umami-packed tomato sauce. Super comfort food that both adults and kids are going to love!

Ingredients

- 4 boneless pork loin chops (1.25 inches thick)

Marinade

- ½ teaspoon (2.3 g) white sugar

- ¼ teaspoon (1.5 g) salt

- ¼ teaspoon (1.25 ml) sesame oil

- 1 tablespoon (15 ml) light soy sauce (not low sodium soy sauce)

- ½ tablespoon (7.5 ml) dark soy sauce

Other Ingredients

- 1 medium onion, sliced

- 4 garlic cloves, minced

- 1 small shallot, diced

- 8 mushrooms, sliced

- 50 ml tomato paste (roughly ⅕ cup)

- 2 tablespoons (30 ml) ketchup

- 1 tablespoon (15 ml) peanut oil

- 1 tablespoon (14 g) white sugar

- 1 teaspoon (5 ml) Worcestershire sauce

- 1 cup (250 ml) of water

- Kosher salt and ground black pepper

- 1 ½ tablespoon (12 g) cornstarch mixed with 2 (30 ml) tablespoons water

How to prepare

- Soften the Pork Chops: With the backend of a weighty knife, pound both sides of the pork chops to soften the meat.

- Marinate the Pork Chops: Marinate the tenderized pork chops for 20 minutes with ½ teaspoon (2.3 g) of sugar, ¼ teaspoon (1.5 g) of salt, ¼ teaspoon (1.25 ml) of sesame oil, 1 tablespoon (15 ml) of light soy sauce, and ½ tablespoon (7.5 ml) of dark soy sauce.

- Prepare the Pressure Cooker: Heat up your pressure cooker (Instant Pot: press Sauté). Make sure your pot is as hot as it can be when you place the pork chops into the pot (Instant Pot: wait until the indicator says HOT). This will stop the pork chops from sticking to the pot.

- Prepare the Other Ingredients: Clean the mushrooms with a damp paper towel and make the rest of the ingredients as listed.

- Sauté the Pork Chops: Add in the peanut oil into the pot. Make sure to coat the oil over the whole bottom of the pot. Add in the marinated pork chops into the pot, then let it brown for roughly 1 − 1 ½ minute on each side (don't need to keep flipping). Do not let it burn. Take out and set aside.

- Brown the Onion, Shallot, Garlic, and Mushrooms: Add in the sliced onions, diced shallot and stir. Add in a pinch of kosher salt and ground black pepper to season if you want. Cook the onions and shallot for about 1 minute until soften. Then, add garlic and stir for 30 seconds until fragrant. Add in the mushrooms and cook for another minute. Taste seasoning and adjust with more kosher salt and ground black pepper if necessary.

- Deglaze: Add in ¼ cup (63 ml) of water and fully deglaze the bottom of the pot with a wooden spoon.

- Create the Tomato Sauce: Add in ¾ cup (188 ml) of water, 2 tablespoon (30 ml) of ketchup, 1 tablespoon (14 g) of sugar, 1 teaspoon (5 ml) of Worcestershire sauce, and 50 ml tomato paste (See Tips). Mix well.

- Pressure Cook the Pork Chops: Place the pork chops back with all the meat juice into the pot. Close lid and pressure cook at High Pressure for 1 minute (Electric and Stovetop Pressure Cookers). Turn off the heat and let it fully Natural Release (roughly 10 minutes). Open the lid carefully.

- Taste & Thicken the Tomato Sauce: Remove the pork chops and set aside. Turn heat to medium (Instant Pot: Press sauté button). Taste the seasoning one more time. Add more salt and pepper if desired. Mix the cornstarch with water and mix it into the tomato sauce one third at a time until desired thickness.

- Serve: Drizzle the tomato sauce over the pork chops and serve immediately with side dishes!

CHAPTER THIRTY THREE

PRESSURE COOKER CHICKEN CONGEE

With 6 simple ingredients and 6 easy steps, make this comforting pressure cooker Chicken Congee in Pressure Cooker. Frugal, healthy & easy one pot meal that is perfect for those busy days.

Ingredients

- ¾ cup (173 g) Jasmine rice (using standard 250 ml cup)

- 6.5 - 7 cups cold water (using standard 250 ml cup)

- 5 – 6 chicken drumsticks

- 1 tablespoon ginger, sliced into strips

- Green onions for garnish

- Salt to taste

How to prepare

- Rinse 173g (3/4 standard cup) of rice in the pot under cold water by carefully scrubbing the rice with your fingertips in a circling motion. Pour out the milky water, and continue to rinse until water is clear. Drain well.

- Add ginger, 5-6 chicken drumsticks and 6.5 - 7 cups of cold water (using standard 250 ml cup) into the pot. Do not add salt at this point. (The ratio is 1 cup rice to 9 - 9.75 cups of water)

- Close the lid right away and cook at high pressure for 30 minutes + Natural Release in an Electric Pressure Cooker.

- Open the lid cautiously. The congee will look runny at this point.

- Heat up the pot (Instant Pot: press Sauté button), stir until desired thickness & consistency. Season with salt.

- Use tongs and fork to break up the chicken meat from the bones (they literally fall off the bone) and take out the chicken bones and skin (if desired).

- Remove congee from heat and garnish with green onions.

- Serve immediately.

CHAPTER THIRTY FOUR

PRESSURE COOKER CREAMY ENCHILADA SOUP

Welcome fall with this calming, veggie packed, healthy, and tasty, easy-to-make Pressure Cooker Creamy Enchilada Soup.

Ingredients:

- 4 cups low sodium chicken broth

- 3 medium size boneless, skinless chicken breasts

- 1 (3.5 ounce) can chopped green chilies

- 1 yellow onion, coarsely chopped

- 3 large russet potatoes, peeled and quartered

- 1 red bell pepper, cored, seeded and coarsely chopped

- 8 cups peeled, cubed butternut squash (about 24 ounces)

- 3 cloves garlic

- 2 teaspoons salt

- 2 teaspoons cumin

- 1 (8 ounce) can tomato sauce

- 2 tablespoons taco seasoning (store bought or homemade recipe to follow)

- 2 (15 ounce) cans cannellini beans, rinsed and drained

- Additional toppings: pico de gallo, sour cream, shredded cheese, fresh or canned corn, diced avocado, Cholula hot sauce, whole grain tortilla chips, etc

Homemade Taco Seasoning

- 1 tablespoon chili powder

- 1 teaspoon ground cumin

- 1 teaspoon garlic powder

- 1 teaspoon smoked paprika

- ½ teaspoon oregano

- ½ teaspoon onion powder

- ¼ teaspoon salt

- ¼ teaspoon black pepper

- ¼ teaspoon crushed red pepper flakes

How to prepare

- Whisk together taco seasoning ingredients if you're using homemade version.

- Add in chicken broth, chicken, green chilies, onion, potatoes, pepper, squash, garlic, salt, cumin, tomato sauce and 2 tablespoons of taco seasoning to the pressure cooker pot and lightly stir.

- Secure the lid and turn pressure release knob to a sealed position. Cook at a high pressure for 20 minutes.

- When cooking is finished, use a natural release. You can also use a natural release for 10 minutes and then discharge any remaining pressure.

- Take out chicken and place on a cutting board, cover with foil. Using an immersion blender, blend soup until very smooth (this can also be done in batches with a blender but be careful not to overfill the blender! Place a towel over the lid and gently pulse before turning the speed up to blend). Chop or shred chicken and return it to the pot of soup. Add cannellini beans and stir.

- To serve, ladle soup into a bowl, immediately sprinkle with cheese and top with desired toppings.

CHAPTER FIVE

PRESSURE COOKER HONEY SESAME CHICKEN

Pressure cooker honey sesame chicken is one of our easy pressure cooker chicken recipes, letting you make your favorite Asian carry-out meals at home! Soft bite size chunks of chicken in a sweet, sticky sauce. This is a quick, easy to make meal that the whole family will love.

Ingredients:

- 4 large boneless skinless chicken breasts, diced (about 2 lbs.)

- Salt and pepper

- 1 tablespoon vegetable oil

- 1/2 cup diced onion

- 2 cloves garlic, minced

- 1/2 cup soy sauce

- 1/4 cup ketchup

- 2 teaspoons sesame oil

- 1/2 cup honey

- 1/4 teaspoon red pepper flakes

- 2 tablespoons cornstarch

- 3 tablespoons water

- 2 green onions, chopped

- Sesame seeds, toasted

How to prepare

- Salt and pepper chicken. Preheat pressure cooking pot using the sauté setting. Add oil, onion, garlic, and chicken to the pot and sauté stirring infrequently until onion is threatened, about 3 minutes.

- Add in soy sauce, ketchup, and red pepper flakes to the pressure cooking pot and stir to mixture. Pressure cook on high for 3 minutes. When timer beeps, turn pressure cooker off and do a quick pressure release.

- Add in sesame oil and honey to the pot and stir to mix. In a small bowl, liquefy cornstarch in water and add to the pot. Select Sauté and simmer until sauce thickens. Stir in green onions.

- Serve over rice sprinkled with sesame seeds.

CHAPTER THIRTY SIX

PRESSURE COOKER MEATBALLS IN EASY TOMATO SAUCE

Make these Pressure Cooker Meatballs soaked in easy tomato sauce. Bursting with smoky flavors and juicy textures, it is a perfect thrifty make a head freezer meal for those hectic weeknights.

Ingredients

Meatballs

- 1 pound (454 g) lean ground beef

- 4 strips bacon (roughly 80 grams), minced

- 1 small onion, roughly chopped

- 4 cloves garlic, roughly minced

- 1 extra large egg, beaten

- 1 teaspoon (1.8 g) dried oregano

- 1 teaspoon (2 g) fennel seed, ground

- ½ teaspoon (2.5 ml) Worcestershire sauce

- ½ teaspoon (1.5 g) kosher salt

- ¼ teaspoon (0.5 g) black pepper

- ½ cup (31 g) panko bread crumbs

- ¼ cup (62.5 ml) milk

- 2 - 2.5oz (60 - 70g) cheese (we used 40 grams freshly grated Parmesan cheese & 30 grams Mozzarella cheese)

Served with Quick & Easy Tomato Sauce

- 2 cups (500 ml) unsalted chicken stock

- 1⅓ cup (398 ml) tomato sauce

- ⅔ cup (156 ml) tomato paste

- 1 teaspoon (1.4 g) basil

- 1 teaspoon (1.8 g) dried oregano

How to prepare

- Mix the Meatballs Ingredients: Mix all the meatballs ingredients in a large mixing bowl. Add the dry ingredients first, then the wet ingredients. Mix well with your hands.

- Make the Easy Tomato Sauce: Combine all the tomato sauce ingredients in your Instant Pot or pressure cooker. Mix well until the tomato paste liquefies into the tomato sauce. Close lid and pressure cook at high pressure for 5 minutes, then Quick Release.

- Preheat Oven & Test Seasoning: While the tomato sauce is cooking, preheat oven to 450°F. Test the seasoning by cooking a small portion of the meatballs mixture on a skillet over medium high heat.

- Roll the Meatballs: Gently roll the meatballs mixture with your hands into ball shapes. As shown in the video, we like to serve ours with the size that is slightly bigger than a golf ball. You should be able to create 8 – 12 meatballs with the listed amount of ingredients.

- Browning in the Oven: Place a piece of parchment paper on your baking tray and gently place the meatballs on it. Place the meatballs in the oven for roughly 12 – 16 minutes until the top is browned but not dried out.

- Pressure Cook the Meatballs: By now, the tomato sauce should be done cooking on the first cycle. Remove the meatballs from the oven and fully submerge the meatballs into the tomato sauce in the Instant Pot or pressure cooker. Close lid and pressure cook at high pressure for another 5 minutes, then quick release.

- Serve: Take out the meatballs from the tomato sauce. Confirm if the internal temperature of the meatballs are at least 145°F.

- Optional: Continue to reduce the tomato sauce until desired consistency. Taste the seasoning of the tomato sauce and add in more salt and pepper if desired. If you like, add more cheese on top of the meatballs when it's served.

CHAPTER THIRTY SEVEN

POTATO LEEK SOUP

Simple and easy potato leek soup, creamy without the cream! Enjoy this tasty, hearty soup with potatoes and leeks.

Ingredients

- 3 pound Russet potatoes peeled large, diced

- 2 leeks white parts only, large, diced

- 1 teaspoon thyme

- 1 teaspoon hot sauce

- 6 cup chicken stock

- 0.5 tablespoon salt

- 0.5 tablespoon White Pepper

- 1 tablespoon olive oil

- 4 ounce Heavy Cream

- 0 chives or scallions

How to prepare

- Position the inner pot into the Pressure Cooker. Press the Soup button. 10 min

- Add the oil; sweat the leeks and celery

- Add in the other ingredients apart from the heavy cream and garnish.

- Position the lid on the Pressure Cooker and Lock. Switch the Pressure Release Valve to Close.

- Once the timer reaches 0, the Cooker will automatically switch to KEEP WARM. Press the CANCEL button. Change the Pressure Release Valve to Open. When the steam is released totally, remove the lid.

- Puree the soup with an emersion blender or cautiously in small batcher in a blender.

- Add in the heavy cream while blending add salt and pepper to taste.

- Serve

CHAPTER THIRTY EIGHT

SOUTHERN SAUSAGE GRAVY

Ingredients

- 1 pound Bulk pork sausage

- 0.25 cup all-purpose flour

- 2 cup Milk (2% or whole)

- 1 tablespoon olive oil

- Salt and pepper to taste

- Pre-made hot biscuits

How to prepare

- Position the Inner Pot into the Pressure Cooker. Press the Rice/Risotto button to set to 6 minutes. Add olive oil.

- Brown the meat. Drain excess fat. Cook garlic and onions.

- Add in all ingredients into the Inner Pot.

- Place the Lid on the Pressure Cooker and lock. Change the Pressure Release Valve to Close.

- Once the Timer reaches 0, the Cooker will automatically switch to KEEP WARM. Press the CANCEL button. Change the Pressure Release Valve to Open. When the steam is totally released, take off the Lid.

- Serve over hot biscuits.

CHAPTER THIRTY NINE

AVOCADO CHICKEN SOUP

This is easy to make, just have all your ingredients diced and chopped before you begin.

Ingredients

- 3 Chicken breasts, diced large

- 6 cup Chicken broth

- 15 ounce Diced tomatoes, drained

- 15 ounce Can of black beans, drained and rinsed

- 1 cup Frozen corn

- 1 Small onion, chopped

- 3 clove garlic, minced

- 0.5 Jalapeno deveined, diced

- 1 teaspoon oregano

- 1 teaspoon cumin

- 0.5 teaspoon Paprika

- Salt and pepper to taste

- 2 tablespoon olive oil

- 2 Limes

- 2 Avocados

- Fresh cilantro, chopped

How to prepare

- Position the Inner Pot in the Cooker. Press the Soup/Stew button to set for 10 minutes.

- Heat the olive oil. Add in the onion and garlic. Cook 2 minutes.

- Add in remaining ingredients except garnish. Stir well.

- Position the Lid on the Cooker. Lock the Lid and switch the Pressure Release Valve to Closed.

- Once the Timer reaches 0, the Cooker will automatically switch to KEEP WARM. Press the CANCEL button. Let the steam naturally release. When the steam is totally released, take off the Lid.

- Garnish with lime juice, diced avocado & cilantro.

- You can also add cooked brown rice, crushed tortilla chips, or grated cheese.

CHAPTER FORTY

SLOPPY JOES

Ingredients

- 2 pound Lean ground beef

- 1 onion, chopped

- 1 cup Green bell pepper, diced

- 8 ounce Can tomato sauce

- 1 tablespoon Brown Sugar

- 2 tablespoon ketchup

- 1 teaspoon Ground mustard

- 1 tablespoon spiced mustard

- 1.5 teaspoon Chili powder

- 1 teaspoon Garlic powder

- 2 tablespoon olive oil

How to prepare

- Place the inner pot into the Pressure Cooker. Press the Rice/Risotto button. Set it to 6 minutes. Add in the Olive Oil and heat.

- Brown the meat drain excess fat and cook garlic and onions

- Add all ingredients into the inner pot.

- Place the lid on the Pressure Cooker and lock. Switch the Pressure Release Valve to Closed.

- Once the timer reaches 0, the Cooker will automatically switch to KEEP WARM. Press the CANCEL button. Switch the Pressure Release Valve to Open. When the steam is released completely, remove the lid.

- Serve

CHAPTER FORTY-ONE

CIOPPINO

Cioppino, a fisherman's fish and shellfish stew from San Francisco, is simple to cook, and delicious with the right ingredients.

Ingredients

- 12 Small hard shell clams, in shell

- 12 Mussels, in shell

- 1.5 pound Raw extra large shrimp, peeled and deveined

- 1.5 pound Fish fillets (halibut, cod, or salmon

- 0.75 cup butter

- 2 Onions, diced

- 3 clove garlic, minced

- 0.5 cup Parsley, minced

- 20 ounce diced tomatoes

- 8 ounce Clam juice

- 1.5 cup White wine

- 2 Bay leaves

- 1 tablespoon Dried basil leaves

- 0.5 teaspoon Dried marjoram leaves

- Salt and pepper to taste

How to prepare

- Place the Inner Pot into the Pressure Cooker. Press the Soup/Stew button. Set for 10 minutes.

- Sweat garlic and onion in the butter.

- Add all ingredients except seafood into the Inner Pot.

- Place the Lid on the Pressure Cooker and lock. Switch the Pressure Release Valve to Closed.

- Once the Timer reaches 0, the Cooker will automatically switch to KEEP WARM . Press the CANCEL button. Switch the Pressure Release Valve to Open. When the steam is released completely, remove the Lid.

- Press the Soup/Stew button to set for 10 minutes (without Lid).

- Add the clams and mussels. Cook for 6-8 minutes.

- Add shrimp and fish. Cook 3-4 minutes until cooked.

CHAPTER FORTY TWO

PUMPKIN SPICE RISOTTO

Pumpkin Spice Risotto with sage is my pick for a simple seasonal fall entree that is loaded with comfort food vibes

Ingredients

- 12 ounce Arborio Rice (Risotto)
- 4 cup chicken stock
- 6 ounce pumpkin puree
- 0.5 onion, diced
- 1 teaspoon thyme, chopped
- 2 clove garlic, minced
- 0.25 teaspoon Nutmeg
- 0.5 teaspoon cinnamon
- 0.25 teaspoon ginger
- 0.25 teaspoon allspice
- 4 ounce Heavy Cream
- 2 ounce olive oil

How to prepare

- Position the Inner Pot into the Pressure Cooker.

- Press the SOUP/STEW button to set for 10 minutes.

- Sauté onion and garlic in olive oil.

- Add in rice and stir. Add in the remaining ingredients.

- Secure the Lid on the Cooker. Lock the Lid and switch the Pressure Release Valve to Closed.

- Once the timer reaches 0, the Pressure Cooker will automatically switch to KEEP WARM. Press CANCEL. Switch the Pressure Release Valve to Open. When the steam is totally released, take off the Lid.

- Fold in heavy cream.

CHAPTER FORTY THREE

POMEGRANATE LEG OF LAMB

This savory roasted lamb is drizzled with an unexpected tangy pomegranate pan sauce just before serving. It's an impressive dish that's ideal for winter or spring entertaining.

Ingredients

- 1 leg of lamb, boneless (tied)

- 1 cup pomegranate juice

- 1 cup White wine

- 1 cup chicken stock

- 0.5 cup pomegranate seeds

- 4 mint leaves

- 4 clove Garlic, peeled and minced

- 1 teaspoon black pepper, ground

- 1 teaspoon Sea Salt

- 3 tablespoon olive oil

- 2 Tbsp. flour

- 2 tsp. butter

- Garnish: 6 mint leaves, Chiffonade; ½ cup pomegranate seeds

How to prepare

- Rub garlic over lamb. Season it with salt and pepper.

- Put the Inner Pot into the Pressure Cooker. Press the MEAT/CHICKEN button. Press the TIME ADJUSTMENT button to set for 20 minutes.

- Place lamb into Inner Pot. Add in olive oil and brown on all sides.

- Add in pomegranate juice. Pour (1/2 cup) pomegranate seeds and mint leaves over lamb.

- Secure the Lid on the Pressure Cooker. Look the Lid the switch the Pressure Release Valve to Closed.

- Once the timer reaches 0, the Pressure Cooker will automatically switch to KEEP WARM. Press CANCEL. Switch the Pressure Release Valve to Open. When the steam is totally released, take off the Lid.

- To make a sauce with drippings, combine butter and flour to form a paste.

- Add in chicken stock and wine to the Inner Pot. Bring it to a boil. Stir in the flour and butter paste. Cook for 5 minutes.

- Garnish with mint and pomegranate seeds.

CHAPTER FORTY FOUR

LOADED MASHED POTATOES

Ingredients

- 4 pound red potatoes, quartered

- 1.5 cup chicken stock

- 1 teaspoon salt

- 0.5 teaspoon pepper

- 1 cup Heavy Cream

- 8 ounce cheddar cheese shredded

- 6 slice bacon, cooked and diced

- 2 ounce butter

- 1 tablespoon parsley chopped

- 2 tablespoon Scallions

How to prepare

- Put the Inner Pot into the Pressure Cooker.

- Press the SOUP/STEW button to set for 10 minutes.

- Add in the potatoes, stock, salt and pepper to the Inner Pot.

- Secure the Lid on the Cooker. Lock the Lid and switch the Pressure Release Valve to Closed.

- Once the timer reaches 0, the Pressure Cooker will automatically switch to KEEP WARM. Press CANCEL. Switch the Pressure Release Valve to Open. When the steam is totally released, take off the Lid.

- Mash the potatoes and add the cream and butter.

- Then fold in the rest of the ingredients,

- Serve

CHAPTER FORTY FIVE

GLAZED CARROT

Turn carrots into a dinner party-worthy side dish with this recipe. It's amazing what a little butter can do to make vegetables taste like dessert--even for picky eaters!

Ingredients

- 2 tablespoon butter, unsalted

- 16 ounce baby carrots

- 4 ounce molasses

- 2 ounce water

- 1 teaspoon salt

- 0.5 teaspoon pepper

- 2 tablespoon dill, chopped

- 2 ounce butter

How to prepare

- Position the Inner Pot into the Pressure Cooker.

- In the Inner Pot, combine carrots, molasses, salt, pepper, and water.

- Secure the Lid on the Pressure Cooker. Lock the Lid and switch the Pressure Release Valve to Closed.

- Press the FISH/VEGETABLE button to set for 2 minutes.

- Once the timer reaches 0, the Pressure Cooker will automatically switch to Keep it warm. Press CANCEL. Switch the Pressure Release Valve to Open. When the steam is completely released, remove the Lid.

- Strain carrots. Add butter to Inner Pot to melt (it will still be warm). Add carrots and dill. Toss delicately.

- Serve with freshly cracked pepper.

CHAPTER FORTY SIX

PRESSURE COOKER BBQ WINGS

If you haven't decided on your dinner menu for Thanksgiving, add this super easy & quick appetizer BBQ Wings to your menu!

Ingredients:

- 2 pounds (907g) Chicken Wings & Drumettes

- ½ cup (125 ml) your favorite BBQ sauce (We used Sweet Ray Original)

How to prepare

- Pressure Cook the Wings: Put 1 cup of cold running tap water and a trivet into the pressure cooker. Put the wings and drumettes on top of the trivet. Close lid and pressure cook at High Pressure for 5 minutes + Full Natural Release Open the lid cautiously.

- Preheat Oven: While the wings and drumettes are natural releasing, preheat oven to 450F.

- Pat Dry the Wings: Remove wings and drumettes from the pressure cooker. Pat it dry with paper towels.

- Apply Sauce and Finish in the Oven: In a large mixing bowl, toss wings and drumettes with ½ cup (125ml) of your favorite BBQ sauce. Place the wings and drumettes in a single layer on a wire rack in a baking tray. Bake until sauce is glossy and caramelized, for 8–15 minutes.

CHAPTER FORTY SEVEN

MOIST AND TENDER PRESSURE COOKER TURKEY BREAST

Turkey breast cooked in the pressure cooker is super moist and soft with only a 30 minute cook time.

Ingredients:

- 6.5 lb. bone-in, skin-on turkey breast

- Salt and pepper, to taste

- 1 (14 oz.) can turkey or chicken broth

- 1 large onion, quartered

- 1 stock celery, cut in large pieces

- 1 sprig thyme

- 3 tablespoons cornstarch

- 3 tablespoons cold water

How to prepare

- Season turkey breast liberally with salt and pepper.

- Put trivet in the bottom of pressure cooking pot. Add chicken broth, onion, celery and thyme. Add the turkey to the cooking pot breast side up. Lock lid in place, select High Pressure and 30 minutes cooking time.

- When beep sounds, turn off pressure cooker and use a natural pressure release for 10 minutes, then do a quick pressure release to release any remaining pressure. When valve drops gently remove lid. Use an instant read thermometer to check to see if the turkey is done. It should be 165°. If it isn't 165°, lock the lid in place and cook it for a few more minutes.

- When turkey has reached 165°, cautiously remove turkey and put on large plate. Cover up with foil.

- Strain and skim the fat off the broth. Whisk corn starch and cold water together; add to broth in cooking pot. Select Sauté and stir until broth thickens. Add salt and pepper to taste.

- Remove and discard the skin. Slice the turkey and serve immediately.

CHAPTER FORTY EIGHT

PRESSURE COOKER PUMPKIN CRÈME BRÛLÉE

This Pressure Cooker Pumpkin Crème Brûlée is classy, creamy custard with the warm, spicy flavors of fall, topped with a thin layer of crispy, caramelized sugar.

Ingredients:

- 6 egg yolks

- 1/3 cup granulated sugar

- 2 tablespoons firmly packed light brown sugar

- 1/4 cup pumpkin puree

- 1 teaspoon vanilla extract

- 2 cups heavy cream

- 1/2 teaspoon cinnamon

- 1/4 teaspoon pumpkin pie spice

- Pinch of salt

- 6 tablespoons superfine sugar

How to prepare

- Put 1 cup of water to the pressure cooking pot and position the trivet in the bottom.

- In a large mixing bowl with a pouring spout, whisk egg yolks, granulated sugar, brown sugar, pumpkin puree, and vanilla together.

- In a small saucepan, whisk together heavy cream, cinnamon, pumpkin pie spice, and salt. Heat over medium heat until cream just begins to seethe.

- Whisking continually, gradually pour the warmed cream mixture into the egg mixture whisking until well blended.

- Pour mixture into six custard cups, cover up with foil, and put three on the trivet in pressure cooking pot. Add in a second trivet and stack the other three cups.

- Lock the lid in place. Select High Pressure and set the timer for 6 minutes. When beep sounds, turn off pressure cooker and use a natural pressure release for 15 minutes and then do a quick pressure release to release any remaining pressure. When valve drops carefully remove lid.

- Carefully remove the cups to a wire rack to cool uncovered. When cool, refrigerate covered with plastic wrap for at least 2 hours or up to 2 days.

- When ready to serve, sprinkle a tablespoon of sugar uniformly over the top of each custard.

- Working with one at a time, move the flame of the torch 2 inches above the surface of each custard in a rounded motion to dissolve the sugar and form a crispy, caramelized topped.

- Substitute 1/2 teaspoon ground cinnamon plus 1/4 teaspoon ground ginger, 1/4 teaspoon ground nutmeg and 1/8 teaspoon ground cloves for 1 teaspoon pumpkin pie spice.

CHAPTER FORTY NINE

PRESSURE COOKER TURKEY STOCK

Pressure Cooker Turkey Stock prepared in your pressure cooker tastes like stock that's been simmered on the stove for hours. But you don't have to skim the foam off the top, nor watch it closely so it doesn't boil too fast, and it cooks in a fraction of the time.

Ingredients:

- 1 roasted turkey carcass, cut into 6 to 8 piece or 2 hindquarters

- 1 large onion, coarsely chopped

- 2 large carrots, roughly chopped

- 2 celery stalks, roughly chopped

- 3 garlic cloves, smashed

- 1 bay leaf

- 5 sprigs fresh parsley

- 3 sprigs fresh thyme

- 1/2 teaspoon whole peppercorns

- 10 cups water

How to prepare

- Pour all of the ingredients in the pressure cooker pot. Select High Pressure and set timer for 30 minutes. When the timer sounds, turn pressure cooker off and use a Natural Pressure release. When valve drops, gently take off the lid.

- Let the stock cool slightly. Pour stock through fine mesh strainer set over a very large bowl or pot. Discard bones, meat, skin, vegetables and herbs. Cover up bowl and refrigerator. When chilled, skim fat from the surface.

CHAPTER FIFTY

PRESSURE COOKER DATE BROWN RICE PUDDING

Ingredients:

- 1 cup short grain brown rice

- 3 cups dairy-free milk (I used cashew milk)

- ½ cup water

- ½ cup pitted dates, cut in small pieces

- 1/8 teaspoon salt

- 1 stick cinnamon

- 1 cup pumpkin puree

- 1 teaspoon pumpkin spice mix

- ½ cup maple syrup

- 1 teaspoon vanilla extract

How to prepare

- Cover up the rice with boiling water and let sit 10 minutes or up to an hour more. Rinse it.

- Bring the milk and water to a boil in a pressure cooker pot. Add in the soaked rice, dates, cinnamon stick, and salt. Lock the lid in place and bring to high pressure for 20 minutes. Use a natural pressure release.

- When the pressure has released, stir in the pumpkin puree, maple syrup, and pumpkin spice mix. Cook, stirring constantly for 3 to 5 minutes, to thicken the pudding and cook out the raw pumpkin flavor. Remove from the heat and discard the cinnamon stick. Stir in the vanilla.

- Transfer to a bowl and cover the surface with plastic wrap, so it touches the hot pudding, to prevent a skin from forming, and so the steam from the hot pudding doesn't condense and create water on the surface. Let cool about 30 minutes. The pudding will thicken as it cools.

- Spoon into serving cups. Serve warm, or cold, topped with maple-syrup sweetened coconut cashew whipped cream or fresh whipped cream. Sprinkle with pumpkin spice mix.

CHAPTER FIFTY ONE

PRESSURE COOKER STUFFING

Quickly "baked" in the pressure cooker and then crisped up in the oven before serving. This Pressure Cooker Stuffing recipe is so simple; you'll want to serve it all year round.

Ingredients:

- 1 1/4 cup turkey or chicken broth

- 1/2 cup butter

- 1 cup celery, chopped

- 1 medium onion, chopped

- 1 loaf bread, cubed and toasted*

- 2 teaspoons salt

- 1 teaspoons sage

- 1 teaspoons poultry seasoning

- 1/4 teaspoon pepper

How to prepare

- Simmer butter, broth, celery and onion until soft. Add in spices. Pour over bread. Mix well.

- Stuff into a 6 cup Bundt pan. Cover it with foil and poke a hole in the middle of the tin foil. Prepare a foil sling for lifting the pan out of the pressure cooker by taking an 18" strip of foil and folding it lengthwise twice.

- Pour in 1 1/2 cups of water into the pressure cooking pot and position the trivet in the bottom. Place the Bundt pan on the centre of the foil strip and lower it into the pressure cooker. Fold the foil strips down so that they do not interfere with closing the lid.

- Lock the lid in place. Choose High Pressure and set the timer for 15 minutes. When beep sounds, turn off pressure cooker and do a fast pressure release to release the pressure. When valve drops carefully lift lid.

- Remove Bundt pan and unmold stuffing on to a foil lined baking tray sprayed with non-stick cooking spray. Put in preheated 350° oven for 5 – 10 minutes to crisp up the stuffing.

- Cube the bread and toast on a rimmed cookie sheet in 350° oven for 20 minutes stirring occasionally. Cool bread before continuing with recipe.

CHAPTER FIFTY TWO

PRESSURE COOKER BUTTERNUT SQUASH BUTTER

Smooth and creamy, this Pressure Cooker Butternut Squash Butter is a pleasant treat for your biscuits, toast and so much more. Fresh ingredients make it naturally tasty, nutritious and appetizing!

Ingredients:

- 6 lbs butternut squash

- 1 cup apple cider

- 1 cup brown sugar, packed

- 2 whole cinnamon sticks

- 1 teaspoon fresh ginger, gratcd

- 1/8 teaspoon nutmeg, grated

- 1/4 teaspoon ground cloves

- 1 tablespoon apple cider vinegar

How to prepare

- Remove the stem and slice off the top and bottom of each squash. Slice in half and remove seeds and stringy fibers. Cut into chunks.

- Pour one cup of water into the pressure cooker pot. Arrange the cut chunks in a steamer basket and place in the pressure cooking pot. Lock the lid in place. Select high pressure and 5 minutes cook time.

- When the pressure cooker has finished cooking and the timer has reached zero, gently release the steam with a quick pressure release. Use hot pads to lift the squash out of the pressure cooker. Let the squash to cool enough to handle.

- Empty the water from the pressure cooker pot, wipe dry and place it back into the cooker. Use a paring knife to remove the skin from the squash.

- Put the cooked, peeled squash into the pressure cooking pot. Add in one cup apple cider and one cup brown sugar. Use a potato masher to mash the squash and mix. Add the cinnamon sticks, ginger, nutmeg, ground cloves and apple cider vinegar to the mixture.

- Lock the lid in place. Choose high pressure and 3 minute cook time. When the pressure cooker has finished cooking and the timer has counted to zero, gently release the steam with a quick pressure release.

- Remove the cinnamon sticks and discard. Use an immersion blender to puree the mixture until smooth. Put into container(s) and cool to room temperature. Refrigerate until ready to serve.

- 2 pounds of cut up winter squash = 2-½ cups of cooked puree.

AIR FRYER COOKBOOK

───── ✥✥✥✥ ─────

Step By Step Guide For Healthy, Easy And Delicious Air Fryer Recipes

John Carter

The information herein is offered for informational purposes solely, and is universal as so. The presentation of the information is without contract or any type of guarantee assurance.

The trademarks that are used are without any consent, and the publication of the trademark is without permission or backing by the trademark owner. All trademarks and brands within this book are for clarifying purposes only and are the owned by the owners themselves, not affiliated with this document.

TABLE OF CONTENTS

CHAPTER 1 143

    WHAT IS AIR FRYER? 143

CHAPTER 2 147

    CONVERTING RECIPES 147

CHAPTER 3 152

    HOW TO COOK FROZEN FOOD IN THE AIR
    FRYER 152

CHAPTER 4 154

    HOW DOES AIR FRYER HELP IN DIETING AND
    WEIGHT LOSS? 154

CHAPTER 5 163

    AIR FRYER RECIPES 163

CHAPTER 6 191

    BREAD AND BREAKFAST 191

CHAPTER 7 199

    MAIN MEALS 199

CHAPTER 8 220

    DESSERTS AND SWEETS...220

CHAPTER 9 240

    SOUP *240*

CHAPTER 1

WHAT IS AIR FRYER?

An air fryer is a kitchen machine that cooks by circling hot air around the food. A mechanical fan courses the hot air around the food at fast, preparing the nourishment and delivering a fresh layer through the Maillard impact.

Conventional browning techniques prompt the Maillard impact by entirely submerging sustenance in hot oil. The air fryer works then again by covering the coveted food in a thin layer of oil while circling air warmed up to 200 °C to give vitality and start the response. By doing this, the machine can broil sustenance like potato chips, chicken, angle, steak, French fries or cakes while utilizing in the vicinity of 70% and 80% less oil than a conventional profound fryer.

Most air fryers accompany adjustable temperature, and clock handles that take into account more precise cooking. Nourishment is cooked in a cooking container that sits on a dribble plate. The container and its substance must occasionally be shaken to guarantee even oil scope; a few models achieve this by consolidating a sustenance fomenter that continually stirs the nourishment amid the cooking procedure while others require the client to play out the errand physically.

Air fryers are alluring for their benefit, security, and medical advantages. A chip fry for gold, with its open best, can without much of a stretch enable hot beads of cooking oil to escape or sprinkle out on the client, which isn't conceivable with an air fryer. Routinely broiled foods are likewise significantly higher in caloric substance, because of the oil retention confident in their arrangement. While proficient gourmet experts have expressed that air fryers complete a great job of making more advantageous copies of pan-fried nourishments, it is likewise, for the most part, concurred that the taste and consistency are not indistinguishable.

How Air Fryer Work?

Air-fryers are independent, windowsill convection stove (so oven with a fan inside), however, with a vertical primer: The fan blows down from the highest point of the gadget through an electric warming component. Wind current begins at best, warms up, at that point surges onto and around your nourishment through a work cooking container, lastly down to a molded dribble plate that recycles the air back to the best. The foodis then suspended amidst this wind current.

That work basket, incidentally, kinda-sorta resembles a profound rotisserie basket,and it's presumably where they got the name. In any case, there's no oil store or anything like that. Indeed, in spite of Philips' claims that you can "broil, barbecue, heat or meal utilizing a tablespoon or less of oil," a few formulas require no oil, or 2 tablespoons, or more. It depends.

Convection stoves and air fryers are fundamentally the same as far as how they cook sustenance, however air fryers are by and large littler than convection broilers and radiate less warmth. Comparable outcomes can be accomplished by utilizing special air crisper plate and placing them under the grill.

The idea behind air fryers is more advantageous, as it aims to bring down fat in cooking. Consolidating hot air, somewhat like a fan appliance, and a little measure of oil, the way they cook,is world-classand far from deep fat fryers which submerge the sustenance in the fat and heap on the calories. However, it's essential to get the correct air fryer as poor ones can abandon you with saturated, tasteless sustenance at the base of the machine – and now and then all through – and you can likewise end up with a device that is hard to work or clean.

Tips for Using an Air Fryer

Shake it.

Make absolute to open the air fryer and shake sustenance around as they "broil" in the machine's crate—littler nourishments like French fries and chips can pack. For best outcomes, pivot them each 4-10 minutes.

Try not to pack.

Nourishing a lot of room so the air can course viable; that is the thing that gives you new outcomes. Our test kitchen cooks swear by the air fryer for bites and little groups.

Give foods a squelch.

Delicately splash foods with acooling shower or include a tad of oil to guarantee they don't adhere to the crate.

Keep it dry.

Pat nourishments dry before cooking (if they are marinated, for instance) to abstain from splattering and abundance smoke. Likewise, when preparing high-fat nourishments, like chicken wings, make a point to discharge the fat from the base machine occasionally.

Ace other cooking strategies.

The air fryer isn't only to fry; it's fantastic for other robust cooking techniques like preparing, simmering and flame broiling, as well. Our test kitchen additionally cherishes to utilize the machine for cooking salmon!

CHAPTER 2

CONVERTING RECIPES

Converting From Traditional Recipes

You can utilize your air fryer to cook recipes that have guidelines for preparing in the grill. Since the heat noticeable all around fryer is more exceptional than a standard stove, diminish the proposed temperature by 24ºF – 40ºF and cut the time by approximately 20%. In this way, if a formula calls for cooking at 400ºF for 20 minutes, air-sear at 370ºF for around 16 minutes.

If you envision that you're cooking a dish supper for Sunday lunch. You have intended to make broil chicken with cook potatoes and vegetables. You would typically steam the vegetables in a skillet and afterward cook the chicken and the potatoes together in the stove; You would then complete dish chicken on the flame broil to fresh up the chicken and vegetables. In any case, now you have an Airfryer and after that exclusive drawback is that it is littler than the space you have in the stove however everything else is fundamentally the same. You would cook the chicken and potatoes together, but since the Airfryer goes about as the prepared, flame broiled and southern style across the board implies that there is less work and less oil included. You can put your chicken and potatoes similarly, at that point you would consist of the oil (however significantly less), and after that, it would cook uniformly and afterward you can serve it.

That chicken and potatoes that would, as a rule, take an hour and a half in the stove will take only 44 minutes in the Airfryer. Add to this that as opposed to splashing the potatoes with a considerable measure of oil to make them fresh you merely require a tablespoon of olive oil for every individual that you are cooking for.

So anticipate that Airfryer cooking will be straightforward and not as troublesome as the way you cook now, so it is a pleasant cooking experience.

Converting from Packaged Foods Directives

A similar manage applies to arranged sustenance that you may purchase at the supermarket. If a pack of solidified French fries proposes cooking in thegrill at440ºF for 18 minutes, air sear the chips at 400ºF and begin checking them at 14 minutes, making sure to shake the crate more than once amid the cooking procedure to enable the chips to darker uniformly.

Using Airfryer to prepare food from packaged food institutions would propel you to wind up testing a great deal to get things right. For instance, few recipes you will discover doesn't require any oil whatsoever, yet a few if you take them to an oil-free formula they can taste shocking. Be that as it may, generally speaking, you should hope to decrease the fat by around 64%.

In case you're an aficionado of KFC Chicken, Chicken Cordon Bleu or Chicken Schnitzel then you will love the oil-free forms for the Airfryer. They suggest a flavor like something that has been crisped and rotisserie when in certainty it has been breaded and made in a considerably more advantageous way.

Expect experimentation however and have a fabulous time formula testing. Our Airfryer French Fries, for instance, took us 3 years to culminate them,and now our meals wouldn't be the same without them!

You can utilize your air fryer to cook formulas that have directions for preparingon the stove. Since the warmth, noticeable all around fryer is more extreme than a standard grill, diminish the proposed temperature by 24°F – 40°F and cut the time by approximately 20%. In this way, if a formula calls for cooking at 400°F for 20 minutes, air-broil at 370°F for around 16 minutes.

Converting to Different Sized Air-Fryers

Bigger air fryers can make life somewhat less demanding, particularly in case you're cooking for at least 4 individuals. Since the bushels in these air fryers are more significant, you can prepare more sustenance at one time and don't need to prepare the nourishment in clusters as determined in a considerable lot of these formulas.Merely recall not to over-fill the air fryer container, since that will directly back off the general cooking time and result in sustenance that is not as fresh as you'd like them to be. What's more, some bigger air fryers with more power may cook food marginally speedier than littler, bring down wattage air fryers. This won't be a unique distinction, yet may spare you 2 or 3 minutes on a few formulas. Similarly, as with everything you cook noticeable all around thefryer, it bodes well to pull open the air fryer combine and check the nourishment as they prepare. That way, you'll maintain a strategic distance from over-cooking anything.

People purchase air fryers primarilybecause they loath to (or have room schedule-wise to, or know how to) cook and a few people just need their broiled treats to be less greasy. The central possibly threatening part is that hurried edibles don't assist with directions for air fryer cooking.

Conversion is a frightening term, yet what's required is entirely straightforward. Air fryers will cook sustenance quicker than an ordinaryoven and needs shaking (shrimp, fries) like a deep fryer does, or flipping and blending, as stove guidelines do.

For impeccability, the readied, covered nourishment is showered with somewhat olive or canola oil, for greatest firmness. Try not to shower a pizza, at all!

Biggerair fryers cook sustenance speedier. Congestion of food anticipates wind current, which backs off cooking time. Moreover, nourishment that is stuffed may not end up noticeably fresh. Instead, it can rise out of your air fryer spongy and baffling.

A 4qt air fryer cooks 2fold the measure of nourishment as a 3qt. The bigger fryer can cook a whole chicken, roast different sustenances on the double and leave space for remains. Ultimately, a 4qt air fryer is basically superior esteem.

Apparently, there are times when a 3qt fryer might be more appropriate. On the off chance that you are cooking for just single or 2 individuals, a 3qt fryer could be perfect. This is particularly valid if you don't need scraps and are not anticipating facilitating extra individuals for future dinners. A 3qt air fryer is additionally better when counter space is constrained. Those on a financial plan may consider the 3qt air fryer as they tend to be more affordable than their more prominent partners.

CHAPTER 3

HOW TO COOK FROZEN FOOD IN THE AIR FRYER

Most pre-arranged foods cook speedier and at higher temperatures than are prescribed for stove warming. When you have changed over and prepared couple, you will have the best of it.

If you have ever managed a conventional oil fryer sometime recently, you know how muddled they can be. Having a hot vat of oil to profound sear your sustenance in can make a wide range of splatters in your kitchen. It can likewise be risky managing hot oil. It isn't phenomenal for individuals who possess oil fryers to get small consumes when oil dots or splatters out of the holder.

In spite of the fact that an advanced profound fryer is intended to dodge splatters, you have to broil legitimately to keep your nourishments from drenching a great deal of oil. Unless you utilize a conventional profound fryer that accompanies an indoor regulator to enable you to get the correct temperature, you may wind up getting oily nourishments. The inordinate oil can be destructive. Then again, air fryers give that same broiled freshness to your sustenance, without suffocating your nourishment in greasy oil.

One way recommended for cooking solidified nourishments in your fryer is utilizing your microwave to defrost it out first before you broil it. That will help abbreviate the critical cooking time that your beforehand solidified sustenance should be in the fryer. It will likewise help expel a portion of the dampness from your solidified nutrition with the goal that it can get decent and fresh in the fryer.

If you will be tossing some solidified meat, veggies, French fries, angle sticks, or potato tots straight into the air fryer, simply remember that they will require a more drawn out time fricasseeing, on the off chance that you didn't defrost them first.

Here Are Some Tips:

- Try not to utilize microwave warming bearings with an air fryer.

- Try not to utilize stove cooking headings as imprinted on the bundle.

- Do shake the bushels as in a profound fryer, or flip the sustenance as you would in a stove.

- Do splash the sustenance with a touch of cooking oil to ensure it crisps.

- You can fill a sustenance safe spritz bottle with your most loved oil. This is said to be better for nonstick surfaces, also.

CHAPTER 4

HOW DOES AIR FRYER HELP IN DIETING AND WEIGHT LOSS?

Dieting or slimming, whatever you call it, is a testing venture, however, it's justified regardless of the exertion. You may feel like you're stuck eating celery sticks and fat-free sustenances and think about whether you'll ever have the capacity to eat something that tastes great again. Are there approaches to appreciate the nourishment you cherish and still stay with your eating regimen?

Possibly you've known about an air fryer and are interested to find out about this progressive kitchen machine. Would it be able to help you with your eating fewer carbs and Weight reduction travel? What are some low-calorie air fryer suppers? What sorts of stable things can the air fryer cook? Is it conceivable to appreciate fricasseed sustenances without all the fat and calories?

In light of Rapid Air Technology, air fryers blow superheated air to cook sustenances that are customarily singed in oil. Regardless of whether you need to make fish sticks and French fries, chicken or even doughnuts, atmosphere that is up to 200 degrees' Celsius starts of course, forming a cooked, fresh surface.

In only 10 to 12 minutes, for example, you can cook a bunch of fries, utilizing significant portion of a spoonful of oil. Furthermore, that is only the start. From cakes to chunks, burgers to steaks, nourishments can be quickly cooked to accomplish similar outcomes when singing, toasting, heating or simmering.

The idea of Air fryerswas at first planned as a more secure, more straightforward technique for searing nourishments, and also diminishing oil-container fires and related wounds. Be that as it may, is this machine more beneficial?

Scientists found that air searing altogether decreased dampness and oil take-up. As far as free unsaturated fats, peroxide esteems and other physicochemical changes, specialists detailed more noteworthy changes in the oil removed from conventional searing techniques, in contrast with air fricasseeing. By and large, scientists presumed that utilizing an air-fryer is, indeed, a more beneficial strategy.

One critical thing to note is the likelihood of expanded free radicals. Regardless of whether little oil is utilized the kind of oil, the temperature, the nourishment that has been cooked and air circulation all impacts the arrangement of free radicals. In case you're a devotee of air browning, in any event, utilize oils that don't oxidize effortlessly, for example, coconut oil.

Before you hop for satisfaction, be that as it may, we have a deplorable yet to include. When taking a gander at the 10,000-foot view, it's smarter to move far from "broiled" sustenances, regardless of whether they're not dug in oil. By the day's end, the foods that air-browning aficionados float towards aren't the most beneficial choices.

As somebody who strives to get thinner and cook sound sustenances, we pondered on similar things. This is what we found about air fryers and Weight reduction. Ideally, the responses to these inquiries can help you on your counting calories and Weight reduction travel.

How Does an Air Fryer Help?

One of the skirmishes of eating fewer carbs is being confined to specific nourishments, especially if those sustenances don't taste great. Entirely disposing of carbs, desserts, singed sustenances, or other delicious things is troublesome and frequently abandons you longing for the things you're endeavoring to stay away from. This makes individuals more inclined to "swindling" on their eating routine and overindulging in unfortunate sustenances.

Cross the thresholdin the air fryer. This kitchen machine gives you the chance to appreciate some of your most loved nourishments, yet healthier. Things like potato chips and French fries cook to fresh, fulfilling flawlessness in an air fryer with practically zero oil and included fat. Changing the way, you prepare nourishments encourages you tostay with your eating regimen and Weight reduction design without giving up the kind of proper sustenance.

Air fryers are a speedy and straightforward approach to cook sustenance at home, where you control precisely what you're eating. They cook an assortment of foodsactively with next to zero oil. This settles on them an excellent decision for individuals who are taking a shot at getting more fit or need to eat substantial suppers. Hence, numerous thinning clubs suggest cooking with an air fryer.

Low-Calorie Meals

Air fryers can cook a wide assortment of sustenances, including chicken, angle, steak, vegetables, pastries, and that's only the tip of the iceberg. Dinners arranged noticeable all around fryer have a tendency to bring down calorie than conventional cooking strategies in light of the fact that the air fryer enables you to accomplish remarkable outcomes with insignificant oil.

Comprehensive Items to Cook in an Air Fryer

It's a snap to cook sound sustenances in an air fryer. A fun aspect concerning this kitchen machine is that it's anything but complicated to explore different avenues regarding and attempt new things. Here are a couple of opinions of sound sustenances that cook well in an air fryer:

- Broiled corn

- Prepared potatoes

- Sweet potato chunks

- Banana chips

- Firm Brussels grows

- Prepared eggs

- Jalapeno poppers

- Cooked carrots

- Vegetable variety

- Green beans with garlic sauce

- Kale chips

- Cooked chickpeas

- Flame broiled pineapple

- Egg and veggie frittata without hull – Season with somewhat salt and pepper and cook in scaled-down pie searches for gold high protein breakfast.

Crab cakes

Burgers – After turning the patties, include a cup of cheddar for whatever is left of the cooking time for a cheeseburger; the cheddar will dissolve onto the patty as it completes the process of cooking.

Chicken quesadillas

Nectar ginger salmon – Marinate salmon in soy sauce, squeezed orange, nectar, minced garlic, minced ginger, and scallions. Prepare at 400 degrees for 9 minutes.

Chicken Parmesan – So tasty you don't miss the breading.

Chicken strips – Dip in egg, at that point daintily bread with Panko pieces. Spritz with olive oil and prepare for 30 minutes at 400 degrees.

Parmesan crusted tortellini

Seared shrimp – Lightly bread, at that point cook to fresh flawlessness and present with mixed drink sauce.

Pork hacks – Marinate in fat-free Italian serving of mixed greens dressing for 2-3 hours, at that point heat for 14 minutes.

Stuffed chime peppers

Lemon pepper chicken – Season chicken, at that point delicately spritz it with olive oil to keep it delicate.

- Chicken wings

- Toasted pumpkin seeds

- Cauliflower tator tots

As should be apparent, there are numerous reliable alternatives with regards to cooking with an air fryer. A most loved substantial side dish is simmered vegetables. Essentially hurl bits of green with little olive oil, season as indicated by taste, and cook at 400 degrees for 8-14 minutes. Broccoli, asparagus, cauliflower, and different vegetables turn out fresh and delightful when cooked along these lines.

Organic product or vegetable chips are another top choice. Daintily cut bananas, carrots, apples, radishes, zucchini, or different products of the soil and place in a single layer broadcasting live fryer plate. Gently season with salt if wanted and heat until it becomes crispy.

Fried Foods with Less Fat and Fewer Calories

Numerous most loved sustenances are browned and loaded with fat, making them untouchable as indicated by most eating routine designs. Notwithstanding, with an air fryer, you can enjoy fresh browned sustenances without the blame. French fries, potato chips, fricasseed chicken, and more are significantly more advantageous when cooked in an air fryer. Appreciate the nourishments you cherish without destroying your eating regimen by changing the way you cook them.

Air fryers use around 80 percent less oil than conventional profound fat fricasseeing. For some broiled sustenances, you can even leave the oil off entirely. Next to zero oil implies that air browned nourishments have far fewer calories and less fat than their conventional partners. Explore different avenues regarding your most loved nourishments to perceive what tastes best to you.

An air fryer is an impressive expansion to the home of anybody endeavoring to get in shape or eat solid nourishment. It's practically no fat cooking technique brings about firm, wonderful broiled nourishments that are much lower in calories, and also extraordinary prepared and simmered sustenances. If there is need for you to appreciate excellent tasting nourishment without destroying your eating routine, an air fryer could be the appropriate response.

It's difficult to cook an assortment of low-calorie dinners and other sound things in an air fryer. Indeed, even fricasseed sustenances aren't beyond reach because of this progressive cooking technique. What are your most loved things to cook in an air fryer? Offer formulas or post any inquiries you have in the remarks.

Try not to deny yourself of all your most loved nourishments with an end goal to stay with a constrained eating routine. Appreciate sound nourishments that taste awesome by changing the way you cook them. Give your eating regimen,and Weight reduction travel a lift by exploring different avenues regarding low-calorie formulas in an air fryer.

Air Fryer and Low Carb

Humans love to feel incredible and look fantastic. For a few people, a low-carb or keto consume fewer calories areconventional method to accomplish this objective. Shockingly, diets like these are limited and may leave you inclining that you can't eat the nourishment you cherish. Are there approaches to keep on enjoying extraordinary tasting nourishments on a low-carb eat less?

Would it be conceivable to make great broiled sustenances that fit with a keto abstain from food? Does cooking at home make it less demanding to stay with an eating routine? Could an air fryer make low-carb nourishments more charming?

With an end goal to answer these inquiries and that's only the tip of the iceberg, researchers set out to take in more of solid low-carb eating and the way toward cooking with an air fryer.

Cooking food for a low-carb or keto abstain from food is trying on occasion. Specific ingredients are confined or forbidden which makes it hard to make the sustenances you cherish. An air fryer can help make things simpler in case you're attempting to take after a unique eating design.

Here are some ways an air fryer supplements a low-carb eat less:

- You can appreciate browned nourishments without the carbs

- It makes cooking at home speedier and less demanding

- Adaptable cooking alternatives keep things fascinating

- Enjoying Fried Foods on a Low-Carb Diet

Singed nourishments are famously undesirable and an improbable piece of any eating routine. Air fryers turn that around. Their progressive cooking technique enables you to accomplish firm, seared nourishments without overabundance oil. This makes it conceivable to appreciate seared nourishments while staying with an eating routine.

Pick a low-carb breading choice when searing sustenance for a keto count calories. Nut flours are a formidable choice for low-carb breading. For some additional surface, attempt finely hacking nuts as opposed to utilizing a nut flour. Splash or hurl sustenances with a saturated or monounsaturated cooking fat like avocado oil, coconut oil, or macadamia oil.

You can put singed sustenances you thought you'd abandoned the keto eating routine back on the menu with an air fryer.

CHAPTER 5

AIR FRYER RECIPES

APPETIZERS

Ricotta Balls with Basil

This Philips Airfryer recipe is a great appetizer for a revelry dinner, or any other occasion.

Ingredients

- 3 slices of stale white bread pepper, freshly ground

- 250 g of ricotta

- 15 g of finely chopped fresh basil

- 2 tablespoons of flour

- 1 separated egg

- 1 tablespoon of finely chopped chives

Guidelines

- Mix everything well together and add 1 tsp of salt and freshly ground pepper, as much as you'd like. After mixing everything, add the chives, the basil, as well as some orange peel.

- You'll be making the balls out of this mixture, so make sure it is well composed.

- Make 20 portions out of the mixture and wet your hands to be able to roll them. Make ball shaped portions and leave them to rest.

- You should preheat your air fryer to 200° C.

- Prepare the bread crumbs out of the bread slices in one bowl, while beating the egg white in another.

- Roll each of the balls into the egg white, and then the bread crumbs.

- Fry the balls 10 by 10, each 10 for 8 minutes.

Air-Fried Beignets

These beignets are scrumptious all alone, yet you can influence chocolate to sauce or raspberry sauce to dress them up on the off chance that you like. To make a super simple and speedy raspberry sauce, mix some raspberry stick with 1 tablespoon of warm water. Thin it just to the consistency you like for plunging.

Ingredients

- A third-quarter filled glass tepid water (around 90°F)

- A quarter-filled glass sugar

- 1 profuse teaspoon dynamic dry yeast

- 3 ½ - 4 glasses useful flour

- A half-filled teaspoon salt

- 2 tablespoons unsalted margarine, room temperature and cut into little pieces

- 1 egg, softly beaten

- A half-filled glass dissipated drain

- ¼ container liquefied spread

- 1container confectioners' sugar

- Chocolate sauce or raspberry sauce, to plunge

Guidelines

- Merge the tepid water, a squeezable amount of the sugar and the yeast in a bowl and let it cook for 4 minutes. It should foam a bit. If it doesn't foam, your yeast isn't dynamic,and you should begin again with new yeast.

- Consolidate 3½ measures of the flour, salt, 2 tablespoons of margarine and the rest of the sugar in a substantial bowl, or in the bowl of a stand blender. Include the egg, garnished drain and yeast blend to the pan and blended with a wooden spoon (or the oar connection of the stand blender) until the point when the mixture meets up in a sticky ball. Include somewhat more flour if essential to get the mixture to shape. Exchange the batter to an oiled bowl, cover with plastic wrap or a perfect kitchen towel and let it ascend in a warm place for no less than two hours or until the point when it has multiplied in mass. Longer is better for enhance advancement, and you can even give the mixture a chance to rest in the fridge overnight (merely make sure to convey it to room temperature before continuing with the formula).

- Roll the mixture out to ½-inch thickness. Cut the dough into rectangular or precious stone molded pieces. You can make the beignets any size you like. However, this formula will give you 24 (2-inch x 3-inch) rectangles.

- Pre-warm the air fryer to 340°F.

- Brush the beignets on the 2 sides with a portion of the softened spread and air-broil in groups at 340°F for 4 minutes, turning them over part of the way through if wanted. (They will darker on all sides without being flipped, yet flipping them will dark colored them all the more equally.)

- When the beignets are done, exchange them to a plate or preparing sheet and tidy with the confectioners' sugar. Serve warm with a chocolate or raspberry sauce.

Baked Ricotta with Lemon and Capers

You could add an egg to this dish and get a puffier outcome - merely ensure you prepare the blend in a straight-sided skillet. To make formula somewhat lighter, you could utilize part-skim ricotta cheddar, yet you'll miss the extravagant lavishness of the cheddar. This is a canapé or bite, so go for the entire drain form and offer it to companions.

Ingredients

- 7-inch pie dish or cake container

- 1½ container entire drain ricotta cheddar or cheese

- Zest of 1 lemon, in plus more for savory

- 1 teaspoon finely hacked new rosemary

- Squeeze pulverized red pepper chips

- 2washed tablespoons

- 2 tablespoons ofadditional virgin olive oil

- Salt and newly ground dark pepper

- 1 tablespoon ground Parmesan cheddar

Ingredients

- Pre-warm the air fryer to 380°F.

- Combine the ricotta cheddar or cheese, lemon get-up-and-go, rosemary, red pepper pieces, olive oil, salt and pepper in a bowl and whisk together well. Exchange to a 7-inch pie dish and place noticeable all around fryer basket. You can utilize aluminum thwart sling to help with this by taking a long bit of aluminum thwart, collapsing it down the middle the long way twice until the point when it would seem that it is around 26-creeps by 3-inches. Place this under the pie dish and hold the finishes of the thwart to move the pie dish all through the air fryer crate. Tuck the finishes of the thwart next to the pie dish while it cooks noticeable all around afryer.

- Air-broil at 380°F for 8 to 10 minutes, or until the point when the best is pleasantly sautéed in spots.

- Expel from the air fryer and promptly sprinkle the Parmesan cheddar to finish everything. Sprinkle somewhat more olive oil to finish everything and include some naturally ground dark pepper and some lemon get-up-and-go as atopping. Serve warm with pita chips or crostini.

Sizzling Air Fryer Turkey Fajitas Platter

You can likewise change this around to white meat you have remaining in your ice chest and you could even do it with extra hotdogs. Also, in light of the fact that it is hacked, prepared and tossed in you can return to putting your feet up or opening a container of wine.

Ingredients

- Philips Airfryer

- 6 Tortilla Wraps

- 100 g Leftover Turkey Breast

- 1 Large Avocado

- 1 Large Yellow Pepper

- 1 Large Red Pepper

- 1 Large Green Pepper

- ½ Small Red Onion

- 5 Tbsp Soft Cheese

- 3 Tbsp Cajun Spice

- 2 Tbsp Mexican Seasoning

- 1 Tsp Cumin

- Salt & Pepper

- Fresh Coriander

Guidelines

- Begin by cutting up your serving of mixed greens. Cleave your avocado into little wedges. Dice your red onion. Cut your peppers into thin cuts.

- Slash up your turkey breast into little pieces.

- Place the turkey, peppers and onions into a bowl and blend with every one of the seasonings alongside the delicate cheddar and afterward put in silver thwart and air broil for 20 minutes on 200c.

- To prevent your turkey from going dry you have to include dampness/fluid to it before you cook it. It's also important that you silver thwart it to again prevent it from going dry.

Spinach and Artichoke White Pizza

You can utilize your most loved locally acquired pizza mixture for this spinach artichoke white pizza formula

Ingredient

- Olive oil

- 3 mugs new spinach

- 2 cloves garlic, minced, partitioned

- 1 (6-to 8-ounce) pizza mixture ball

- ½ glass ground mozzarella cheddar

- ¼ glass ground Fontina cheddar

- ¼ glass artichoke hearts, coarsely hacked

- 2 tablespoons ground Parmesan cheddar

- ¼ teaspoon dried oregano

- Salt and crisply ground dark pepper

Guidelines

- Heat the oil in medium sauté container on the stovetop. Include the spinach and a significant portion of the minced garlic to the dish and sauté for a couple of minutes, until the point that the spinach has withered. Expel the sautéed spinach from the container and put it aside.

- Pre-warm the air fryer to 390°F.

- Cut out a bit of aluminum thwart an equal size from the base of the air fryer basket. Brush the thwart hover with olive oil. Shape the batter into a circle and place it over the thwart. Dock the mixture by puncturing it a few times with a fork. Brush the paste daintily with olive oil and move it into the air fryer container with the thwart on the base.

- Air-fry the plain pizza mixture for 6 minutes. Turn the mixture over, expel the aluminum thwart and brush again with olive oil, air-broil for an extra 4 minutes.

- Sprinkle the mozzarella and Fontina cheeses over the mixture. Top with the spinach and artichoke hearts. Sprinkle the Parmesan cheddar and dried oregano to finish everything and shower with olive oil. Lower the temperature of the air fryer to 340°F and cook for 8 minutes, until the point that cheddar has softened and is delicately caramelized. Season to taste with salt and new ground dark pepper.

Tandoori Chicken

Tandoori Chicken Recipe is a lip-smacking dry chicken dish from the Indian subcontinent, and it happens to be that one dish that a gathering or assembling just can't manage without. Chicken marinated in flavors till it gets the profound, dynamic look and taste, and from there on cooked in an Indian style.

Ingredients

- 4 Chicken legs
- For the first Marinade
- Ginger paste - 3 tsp
- Garlic paste - 3 tsp
- Salt to taste
- Lemon juice - 3 tbsp
- For the second Marinade
- Tandoori masala powder - 2 tbsp
- Roasted cumin powder - 1 tsp
- Garam masala powder - 1 tsp
- Red chili powder - 2 tsp
- Turmeric powder - 1 tsp
- Hung curd - 4 tbsp

- Orange food color - a pinch

- KasuriMethi - 2 tsp

- Black pepper powder - 1 tsp

- Coriander powder - 2 tsp

Guidelines

- Wash the chicken legs and make openings in them utilizing a sharp blade.

- Include the chicken in a bowl alongside the elements for the principal marinade.

- Blend well and keep aside for 15 minutes.

- Blend the elements for the second marinade and pour them over the chicken.

- Cover the bowl and refrigerate for no less than 10-12 hours.

- Line the bushel of the air fryer with aluminum foil.

- Pre warmth to 230 degrees C.

- Place the chicken on the bushel and air broil for 18-20 minutes, until somewhat scorched and cooked.

- Serve hot with Yogurt mint plunge and Onion rings

Air Fryer Baked Garlic Parsley Potatoes

Air Fryer Baked Potato shrouded in a parsley garlic salt rub. You'll never eat a plain baked potato again!

In case you're here to figure out how to prepare a potato you're in the correct spot. The air fryer baked potatoes are such a great amount of superior to making a baked potato in the stove. When you put on the seasonings it just takes the potatoes to another level.

Mac and Cheese

Ingredients:

- 2 cups of dry macaroni of your choice

- 2 cups of shredded cheddar cheese

- 1 tsp of corn starch

- 2 cups of heavy whipping cream

Guidelines

- Add the corn starch and half the cup of cheese in a bowl and mix them well with all the other ingredients.

- Add the mixture into the baking pan of your air fryer and cover with foil.

- Now, add the pan into the frying basket. Most of the air fryers have a bake setting. Choose if available.

- Cook the mixture for approximately 15 minutes, at 310 degrees.

- After 15 minutes, remove the foil and add the rest of the cheese.

- Continue the baking process for another 10 minutes, at the same temperature

Ingredients

- 3 Idaho or Russet Baking Potatoes

- 1-2 Tablespoons Olive Oil

- 1 Tablespoon Salt

- 1 Tablespoon Garlic

- 1 Teaspoon Parsley

Guidelines:

- Wash your potatoes and after that make air openings with a fork in the potatoes.

- Sprinkle them with the olive oil and seasonings; at that point rub the seasoning equitably on the potatoes.

- Once the potatoes are covered place them into the bushel for the Air Fryer and place into the machine.

- Cook your potatoes at 392 degrees for 35-40 minutes or until the point that fork delicate.

- Top with your top picks. We cherish new parsley and sour cream

Air Fryer Falafel Balls

Air Fryer Falafel Balls are crunchy outwardly, delicate within, and idealize on plates of mixed greens or stuffed into a pita. Shower with custom made tahini dressing.

Ingredients

- 2 tablespoons olive oil

- 1/2 cup diced sweet onion

- 1/2 cup minced carrots

- 1/2 cup roasted salted cashews

- 1 cup rolled oats

- 2 cups cooked or 1, 15 ounce can-sealed chickpeas

- 2 tablespoon soy sauce

- juice of 1 fresh lemon

- 1 tablespoon flax meal

- 1 teaspoon each ground cumin and garlic powder

- 1/2 teaspoon turmeric

Guidelines

- In an extensive skillet, warm the olive oil on medium high warmth. Cook the onions and carrots until the point that they mollify, around 7 minutes, at that point exchange them to an expansive bowl.

- Put the cashews and oats into your sustenance processor and crush until the point that you get a coarse dinner. Add that to the bowl with the veggies.

- Put the chickpeas into your sustenance processor with the soy sauce and lemon squeeze and puree until they're semi-smooth (a few pieces are thoroughly alright). You'll presumably need to stop and rub down the side a couple of times to get things moving. Exchange those to a similar bowl, at that point mix in the flax and flavors. Ensure everything is fused extremely well, and utilize a fork to squash up any enormous bits of chickpeas that you experience while you're mixing. It's fine in the event that you don't crush each and every chickpea. This formula is extremely lenient.

- Utilize your hands to make 12 falafel balls from the mixture, at that point organize them in a solitary layer in your air fryer bushel.

- Cook at 370 for 12 minutes, shaking following 8 minutes.

- Serve stuffed into a wrap or over plate of mixed greens with Magical Tahini Dressing.

Fried Green Tomatoes with Sriracha Mayo

This formula is best made in the late spring when tomatoes are in season, and most stores convey green vegetables (tomatoes precisely) or even better pick them right on time from your particular garden. A primary and decent approach to dress these up is to top each completed fricasseed tomato cut with some fresh crabmeat and shower the sriracha mayonnaise to finish everything.

Ingredients

- 3 green tomatoes

- Salt and newly ground dark pepper

- 1-third of container flour

- 2 eggs

- ½ container buttermilk

- 1 container of breadcrumbs

- 1 container of cornmeal

- New thyme sprigs or cleaved fresh chives

- Sriracha Mayo:

- ½ container mayonnaise

- 1 to 2tablespoons hot sriracha sauce

- 1 tablespoon drain

Guidelines

- Cut the tomatoes in ¼-inch cuts. Pat them dry with a cleanscullerycloth and season liberally with salt and pepper.

- Set up a digging station utilizing 3 shallow dishes. Place the flour in the main shallow bowl, consolidate the eggs and buttermilk in the second plate, and join the flour and cornmeal in the third recipe.

- Pre-warm the air fryer to 400°F.

- Dig the tomato cuts in flour to coat on the 2 sides. At that point dunk them into the 9egg blend lastly squeeze them into the breadcrumbs tocover all sides of the tomato.

- Splash or brush the air-fryer bushel with olive oil. Exchange 3 to 4 tomato cuts into the container and shower the best with olive oil. Air-broil the tomatoes at 400°F for 8 minutes. Flip them over, shower the opposite favor oil and air-fry for an extra 4 minutes until brilliant darker.

- While the tomatoes are cooking, make the sriracha mayo. Consolidate the mayonnaise, 1 tablespoon of the hot sriracha sauce and drain in a little bowl. Mix well until the point when the blend is smooth. Add more sriracha sauce to taste.

- At the point when the tomatoes are done, exchange them to a cooling rack or a platter fixed with paper towels, so the base does not get spongy. Before serving, painstakingly stack the every one of the tomatoes into air fryer and air-broil at 340°F for 1 to 2 minutes to warm them go down.

- Serve the fried green tomatoes hot with the sriracha mayo as an afterthought. Season 1 final time with salt and naturally ground dark pepper and embellishment with sprigs of fresh thyme or hacked fresh chives.

Sockeye Salmon en Papillote with Potatoes, Fennel & Dill

Ingredients

- 2 to 3 fingerling potatoes, daintily cut ¼-inch thick

- ½ globule fennel, meagerly sliced ¼-inch thick

- 4 tablespoons spread, liquefied

- Salt and newly ground dark pepper

- New freshdill

- 2 (6-ounce) sockeye salmon filets

- 8 cherry tomatoes split

- Quarter-filled container dry vermouth (or white wine or fish stock)

Guidelines

- Pre-warm the stove (or air fryer) to 400°F.

- Heat a little pot of salted water to the point of boiling. Whiten the potato cuts for 2minutes until they merely begin to mollify marginally. Deplete and dry with a spotless kitchen towel.

- Cut out 2 expansive rectangles of material paper – around one 3-creep by 14-inches each. Hurl the potatoes, fennel, half of the dissolved spread, salt and newly ground dark pepper together in a bowl. Partition the vegetables between the 2 bits of material paper, setting the vegetables on one portion of every rectangle. Sprinkle some crisp dill to finish everything.

- Place a filet of salmon on each heap of vegetables. Season the fish exceptionally well with salt and pepper. Hurl the cherry tomatoes to finish everything. Sprinkle the rest of the margarine over the fish. Separation the vermouth between the 2 bundles, showering it over the fish.

- Crease up every material square by first collapsing the rectangles into equal parts over the fish. Beginning at one corner, make a progression of straight overlays on the external edge of the squares to seal the edge together.

- Place the 2 bundles onto a heating sheet and prepare in the 400°F oven for 14 to 20 minutes. (Or then again, cook one bunch at any given moment noticeable all around fryer for 10 minutes each.) The bunch ought to be puffed up and marginally fried when thoroughly cooked. The fish should feel firm to the touch (you can frequently, deliberately, push on the fish through the paper).

- You can serve these primarily with the material paper efficiently slice open to uncover the internal parts, have your guests cut open the bundles at the table, or evacuate the material totally, exchanging the top-notch inner pieces to a plate. Sauce with somewhat more fresh dill.

Pickle-Brined Fried Chicken

This is a scrumptious singed chicken recipe that utilizes the saline solution left in the pickle jostle when you've completed every one of the pickles. This formula calls for legs, however,if you favor white meat, don't hesitate to substitute bone-in chicken bosoms.

Ingredients

- 4 chicken legs (bone-in and skin-on), cut into drumsticks and thighs (around 3½ pounds)

- Pickle juice from a 24-ounce jug of genuine dill pickles

- Half-filled glass of flour

- Salt and naturally ground dark pepper

- 2 eggs

- 2 tablespoons vegetable or canola oil

- 1 fine glass breadcrumbs

- 1 teaspoon salt

- 1 teaspoon typicallygrated dark pepper

- ½ teaspoon ground paprika

- ⅛ teaspoon cayenne pepper

- Vegetable or canola oil in a shower bottle

Guidelines

- Place the chicken in a shallow dish and pour the pickle squeeze over the best. Cover and exchange the chicken in the fridge to salt water in the pickle juice for 3 to 8 hours.

- When you are prepared to cook, expel the chicken from the fridge to give it a chance to come to room temperature while you set up a rigging station.Place the flour in a trivial dish and season well with salt and crisply ground dark pepper. Whisk the eggs and vegetable oil together in a moment shallow dish. In a third shallow dish, consolidate the breadcrumbs, salt, pepper, paprika and cayenne pepper.

- Pre-warm the air fryer to 370°F.

- Expel the chicken from pickle brackish water and tenderly dry it with a perfect kitchen towel. Dig each bit of chicken in the flour, at that point dunk it into the egg blend, lastly squeeze it into the breadcrumb blend to coat all sides of the chicken. Place the breaded chicken on a plate or preparing sheet and splash each piece done with vegetable oil.

- Air-broil the chicken in 2 clusters. Place 2 chicken thighs and 2 drumsticks into the air fryer bushel. Air-broil for 10 minutes. At that point, delicately turn the chicken pieces over and air broil for an additional 10 minutes. Expel the chicken pieces and let them lay on theplate – don't cover. Rehash with the second cluster of chicken, air browning for 20 minutes, turning the chicken over part of the way through.

- Lower the temperature of the air fryer to 340°F. Place the central clump of chicken over the second group as of now in the crate and air broil for an extra 7 minutes. Warm and enjoy.

Air-Fried Turkey Breast with Maple Mustard Glaze

How awesome that you can cook a turkey bosom in your air fryer! That implies that you can prepare an extra heartin caseyou have a tremendous group for thanksgiving, or in case you're having a little gathering, you can air-broil your turkey and leave your stove accessible for all the side dishes. You'll need a considerable air fryer for this formula - no less than 4 quarts in themeasure. If you have alittle air fryer, you can attempt a boneless 3-pound turkey breast and cook it for around 30 −4 to 4 minutes

Ingredients

- 2 teaspoons olive oil

- 4-pound entire turkey bosom

- 1 teaspoon dried thyme

- ½ teaspoon drained sage

- ½ teaspoon smoked paprika

- 1 teaspoon salt

- ½ teaspoon newly ground dark pepper

- ¼ container maple syrup

- 2 tablespoon Dijon mustard

- 1 tablespoon butter

Guidelines

- Pre-warm air fryer to 340°F.

- Brush the olive oil everywhere throughout the turkey bosom.

- Consolidate the thyme, sage, paprika, salt,and pepper and rub the outside and visible part of the turkey bosom with the zest blend.

- Exchange the prepared turkey bosom to the air fryer crate and air-fry at 340°F for 24 minutes. Turn the turkey bosom on its side and air-fry for an additional 12 minutes. Turn the turkey bosom on the contrary side and air-broil for an extra 12 minutes. The inside temperature of the turkey bosom should achieve 164°F when thoroughly cooked.

- While the turkey is air-frying, consolidate the maple syrup, mustard and spread in a little pan. At the point when the concocting time is, restore the turkey bosom to an upright position and brush the coating everywhere throughout the turkey. Air-broil for a last 4 minutes, until the point when the skin is pleasantly cooked and fresh. Give the turkey a chance to rest, approximately rose with thwart, for no less than 4 minutes before cutting and serving.

CHAPTER 6

BREAD AND BREAKFAST

Peach Crisp

Ingredients

- 4 cups of sliced peaches, frozen

- 3 Tablespoon sugar

- 2 Tablespoon Flour, white

- Teaspoon sugar, white

- 0.25 cup Flour, white

- 0.33 cup oats, dry rolled

- 3 tablespoon butter, unsalted

- 1 teaspoon cinnamon

- 3 tablespoon pecans, chopped

Guidelines

- In a bowl, mix the peaches with 3 Tbsp. sugar, 2 Tbsp. flour and 1 tsp. cinnamon. Pour into the Baking Pan.

- Place the Baking Pan into the Fry Basket.

- Secure the Fry Basket inside the Power Air Fryer XL.

- Set time & temperature manually to 20 minutes at 300 degrees.

- Half way through cooking, give the peaches a stir.

- In a bowl mix the rest of the ingredients to make the crisp topping.

- When the time runs out on the peaches, remove the Fry Basket and top with the crisp topping.

- Place the Fry Basket back into the Power Air Fryer XL.

- Press the Power Button & adjust cooking time to 10 minutes at 310 degrees and Bake.

- When the crisp is done, let cool for 15 minutes. Serve with your favorite ice cream.

Fish Tacos

Ingredients:

- 10 ounces of cod filet

- 1 cup of Panko

- 6 flour tortillas

- 1 cup of tempura batter

- 1 cup of cole slaw

- 0.5 cup of salsa

- 1 tsp of white pepper

- 0.5 cup of guacamole

- 2 tbsp of chopped cilantro

- 1 lemon cut into wedges

- Power XL Air Fryer

Guidelines:

- Make the tempura batter by mixing 1 cup of flour, 1 tbsp of cornstarch, and half a cup of seltzer water cold.

- Add some salt to the mixture, and make it smooth.

- Cut the Cod filets into long 2 oz pieces. After doing so, season each piece with pepper and salt.

- Use the previously made batter to cover the pieces. Dredge them in the panko.

- Add the pieces into the air fryer basket.If your air fryer comes with a French Fry setting, choose that button.

- The estimated frying time is 10 minutes. After 5 minutes, turn the pieces.

- Once they're ready, put a piece on a tortilla with guacamole, cole slaw, salsa, and a spritz of lemon juice. You can also add the chopped cilantro.

Monte Cristo Sandwich

A Monte Cristo sandwich is a "French toasted ham and cheddar sandwich." It has the sweet taste of French toast with the salty kind of the ham and Swiss cheddar to make a truly divine blend. It's presented with powdered sugar and an organic product safeguard, yet there are such a large number of varieties of the sandwich that it's honestly up to you how you'd get a kick out of the chance to serve it.

Ingredients

- 1 egg for omelets

- 3 tablespoons creamer

- ¼ teaspoon vanilla concentrate

- 2piecesof sourdough, white or multigrain bread

- 2½ ounces cut Swiss cheddar

- 2ounces' cuts store ham

- 2 ounces cut store turkey

- 1 teaspoon margarine, dissolved

- Powdered sugar

- Raspberry stick, for serving

Guidelines

- Mix the egg, cream and vanilla flavor in a shallow bowl.

- Place the bread on the counter. Construct a sandwich with one cut of Swiss cheddar, the ham, the turkey and after that a moment cut of Swiss cheddar on one cut of the bread. Top with the other cut of dough and press down marginally to straighten.

- Pre-warm the air fryer to 340°F.

- Cut out a bit of aluminum thwart about an indistinguishable size from the bread and brush the thwart with dissolved margarine. Plunge the 2 sides of the sandwich into the egg hitter. Give the hitter a chance to drench into bread for around 30 seconds on each side. At that point put the sandwich on the lubed aluminum thwart and exchange it to the air fryer container. For additional frying, brush the highest point of the sandwich with thedissolved spread. Air-fry at 340°F for 10 minutes. Flip the sandwich over, brush with spread and air-broil for an extra 8 minutes.

- Exchange the sandwich to a serving plate and sprinkle with powdered sugar. Present with raspberry as an extra enjoyment.

Pumpkin and Sunflower Seed Soft Bums Fruit Cake Air Fry Bread

Have you ever consider baking your homemade crisp bread? It's not a smart thought in light of the fact that, with your air fryer, you can accomplish more than heat a cake and basic dinners with fruits.

Ingredients

- 215 grams flour

- 30 grams sugar

- 100 grams of fresh milk)

- 30 grams of butter

- 1/3 egg

- 1 teaspoon of instant yeast

- 1 teaspoon of salt

Guidelines:

- Right off the bat, every one of the ingredients without butter ought to be combined. At the point when the blend's smooth and versatile, then add the butter spread at that point keep on mixing them.

- Now the bread ought to be sealed in 2 hours 45 minutes to have the batter twofold in measure. From that point onward, it ought to be secured with a top or stick wrap.

Additionally, you ought to keep all the breeze from become scarce the bread.

- Here, the mixture ought to be separated into balls of 25 grams and rest them for around 10 minutes.

- Blend the egg yolk with drain or water to have the egg wash.

- Presently, you simply need to shape the blend into the ball and put them on the preparing paper. You can have an alternate shape as you need. From that point forward, cover them with egg wash above.

- From that point onward, the mixture needs sealing again in 45 minutes to have multiplied in measure and have every one of them in a warm condition.

- After about 45 minutes, take it out and splash them with a water to give additional dampness. At that point, heat them in the air fryer at 160 degrees C for 5 minutes.

- All things considered, you simply need to brush the bun with some margarine and appreciate it.

- While blending the ingredients, you ought to do until the point when they are not stickier but however, glossy and smooth. Likewise, please keep all the breeze from the mixture to be not dry them and you can accelerate the sealing time by a kitchen with hotter temperature

CHAPTER 7

MAIN MEALS

Black Cod with Grapes, Fennel, Pecans and Kale

Dark cod is otherwise called sablefish or butterfish. It's not quite of the cod family and not like cod in flavor or surface. It's rich and nutritious and has more sound omega-3 unsaturated fats than some other white fish.

Ingredients

- 2 (6-to 8-ounce) filets of dark cod (or sablefish)
- Salt and newly ground dark pepper
- Olive oil
- 1 container grapes, split
- 1 little knob fennel, cut ¼-inch thick
- ½ glass pecans
- 3 mugs of threadbare kale
- 2 teaspoons white balsamic vinegar or white wine vinegar
- 2 tablespoons additional virgin olive oil

Guidelines

- Pre-warm the air fryer to 400° F.

- Season the cod filets with salt and pepper and sprinkle, spread or shower a little olive oil to finish everything. Place the fish, introduction side up (skin side down), into the air fryer bushel. Air-broil for 10 minutes.

- At the point when the fish has got done with cooking, evacuate the filets to a side plate and freely tent with thwart to rest.

- Hurl the grapes, fennel and pecans in a bowl with a shower of olive oil and season with salt and pepper. Include the grapes, fennel and pecans to the air fryer container and air-broil for 4 minutes at 400°F, shaking the bushel once amid the cooking time.

- Exchange the grapes, fennel and pecans to a bowl with the kale. Dress the kale with the balsamic vinegar and olive oil, season to taste with salt and pepper and serve close by the cooked fish.

Quinoa Burgers

These quinoa burgers are fulfilling and pack a punch of protein.

Ingredients

- 1 glass quinoa (red, white or multi-shaded)

- 1½ glasses water

- 1 teaspoon salt

- Naturally ground dark pepper

- 1½ glasses moved oats OR entire wheat breadcrumbs

- 3 eggs, gently beaten

- ¼ glass minced white onion

- ½ glass disintegrated feta cheddar

- ¼ glass cleaved new chives

- Salt and naturally ground dark pepper

- Vegetable or Canola oil

- Whole wheat ground sirloin sandwich buns

- Tomato piece

- Cucumber dill yogurt sauce

Guidelines

- Make the quinoa: Rinse the quinoa in icy water in a pot, twirling it with your hand until the point that any dry husks ascend to the surface. Deplete the quinoa and also you can and afterward put the pan on the stovetop. Turn the warmth to medium-between a rock and a hard place the quinoa on the stovetop, shaking the container routinely until the point when you see the quinoa moving effectively and can hear the seeds moving in the skillet. Include the water, salt and pepper. Heat the fluid to the point of boiling and afterward decrease the warmth to low or medium-low. You should simply observe a couple of air pockets, not a bubble. Cover with a top, abandoning it to one side (or on the off chance that you have pour gushes, simply put the top on the pot) and stew for 20 minutes. Subsidize the heat and cushion the quinoa with a fork. In the event that there's any fluid left in the base of the pot, put it back on the burner for an additional 3 minutes or somewhere in the vicinity. Spread the cooked quinoa out on a sheet skillet to cool.

- Conglomerate the room temperature quinoa in a huge bowl with the oats, eggs, onion, cheddar and herbs. Season with salt and pepper and amalgam well. Shape the blend into 4 patties. Include a little water or a couple of more moved oats to persuade the blend to be the correct consistency to make patties.

- Pre-warm a sauté container over medium warmth. Add enough oil to cover the base of the skillet. Add the quinoa burgers to the container. Cover and let the burgers cook for 4 minutes. Check the base of the burger to ensure it has caramelized pleasantly. Flip the burger over, cover and cook for another 4 to 7 minutes, or until the point that the 2 sides are pleasantly sautéed.

- Air Fryer Instructions: Cascade the 2 sides of the patties liberally with oil and exchange them to the air fryer container in one layer (It is most likely that there will be need to cook these burgers in bunches relying upon the extent of the air fryer). Air-fry each group at 400°F for 10 minutes, flipping the burgers over part of the way through the cooking time.

- Make the burger all in all wheat ground sirloin sandwich buns with arugula, tomato and the cucumber dill yogurt sauce.

Air Fryer Drumsticks: Healthier Fried Chicken

It appears to be wrong that wings get the majority of the consideration when these Air Fryer Drumsticks are fit for an eatery banquet.

Grill nourishment gets a minor adjustment with an air fryer that prompts generous calorie investment funds and considerably more adjusted sustenance. The normal drumstick sees its wellbeing esteem decrease quickly, showered in oil, broiled and regularly bundled in a family-estimate basin no individual could vanquish. This air fryer recipe has your health opulence as a top priority, while additionally taking into account your most profound, darkest chicken longings. Cajun seasoning adds a pow of dramatization to this dish, which includes more satisfying meat on the bone than firm outside covering included.

Air Fryer Drumsticks are one Powerful with one Extra kick of astounding per serving. Appreciate them as seems to be, or pair them with a solid grain like darker rice for an awesome begin to a flex lunch.

Ingredients

- 2 chicken drumsticks, skin removed

- 2 tsp. olive oil

- 1 Tbsp. Cajun seasoning

- 1 Tbsp cayenne pepper

- 1 Tbsp paprika

- 1 Tbsp garlic powder

- 1 Tbsp onion powder

- 1 Tbsp oregano

Guidelines

- Consolidate olive oil and Cajun seasoning for marinade in an enclosed satchel.

- Include chicken and let it marinate for no less than 30 minutes.

- Preheat air fryer to 400° F.

- Exchange chicken to air fryer container and cook for another 15 minutes

Eggplant Parmesan Panini

There are a couple of ventures to making this Panini, yet it's justified, despite all the trouble at last. It takes every one of the kinds of Eggplant Parmesan and places it in a generous Panini! Salting eggplant before cooking may remove a chemical that tends to give eggplant an intense taste (there's much level headed discussion on this), however more critically it coaxes dampness out of the eggplant abandoning you with a lovelier and less stringy surface. Despite that it might appear to be disturbance to sprinkle a considerable measure of salt on the eggplant, rest guaranteed that you brush a large portion of the salt off the cuts previously cooking it, and your eggplant will be prepared flawlessly.

Ingredients

- 1 medium eggplant (around 1 pound), cut into ½-inch cuts

- Genuine salt

- ½ glass breadcrumbs

- 2 teaspoons dried parsley

- ½ teaspoon Italian flavoring

- ½ teaspoon garlic powder

- ½ teaspoon onion powder

- ½ teaspoon salt

- Crisply ground dark pepper

- 2 tablespoons drain

- ½ glass mayonnaise

- 4 cuts craftsman Italian bread

- ¾ glass tomato sauce

- 2 glasses ground mozzarella cheddar

- 2 tablespoons ground Parmesan cheddar or cheese

- Slashed crisp basil

Guidelines

- Set up the eggplant by liberally salting the 2 sides of the eggplant cuts and laying them level between sheets of paper towel. Give the eggplant a chance to sit like this for 30 minutes while you set up whatever is left of the formula ingredients.

- Set up anexcavating station. Consolidate the breadcrumbs, parsley, Italian flavoring, garlic powder, onion powder, salt and dark pepper in a shallow dish. Whisk the drain and mayonnaise together in a little bowl until smooth.

- Pre-warm the air fryer to 400°F.

- Brush the abundance salt from the eggplant cuts and afterward coats the 2 sides of each cut with the mayonnaise blend. Dunk the eggplant into the breadcrumbs, squeezing the morsels onto the eggplant to coat the 2 sides of each cut. Place all the covered eggplant cuts on a plate or preparing sheet and shower the 2 sides with olive oil. Air-fry the eggplant cuts in clusters for 14 minutes, turning them over part of the way through the cooking time.

- When the greater part of the eggplant has been fried, amass the Panini. Liberally brush 1 side of each cut of bread with olive oil. Place 2 cuts of bread on a cutting board, oiled side down. Top each cut with a 4th of the mozzarella cheddar and sprinkle with some Parmesan cheddar. Gap the cooked eggplant between the 2 Panini, putting them on the cheddar. Spoon the tomato sauce equitably finished the eggplant and best with residual mozzarella and Parmesan cheeses. Sprinkle with the hacked crisp basil and place the second cuts of bread to finish everything, oiled side up.

- Place sandwiches onto a pre-warmed contact barbecue or Panini press and close the cover, push down somewhat to ensure bread will dark colored equally. Flame broil for 10 minutes until the point that bread is toasted and cheddar is dissolved. On the other hand, flame broils the Panini in a barbecue dish with a Weighted push to finish everything and flip it over part of the way through cooking.

- Restore the completed cooked Panini to a cutting board and let them rest for 1 to 2 minutes. At that point, cut every down the middle and serve quickly.

Air Fryer Coconut Shrimp with Spicy Apricot Sauce

This fabulously sweet and crunchy formula is perfect for couples endeavoring to get fit as a fiddle by practicing good eating habits. Shrimp is a low-calorie type of protein you'll hunger for quite a long time when it's covered in tropically sweet coconut and made into crunchy bits of paradise in the air fryer. Avoid the rotisserie applications at the nearby bar, for a natively constructed take that beats its opposition anytime. Addicting doesn't start to portray this Air Fryer Coconut Shrimp, which is only 250 calories and, when utilizing precooked shrimp, is done in five minutes!

Since this great dish considers a large portion of a SmartCarb, one PowerFuel and two Extras, it is amazingly adaptable. Appreciate it as a between-feast nibble or as a base for a flex supper. In the event that you appreciate it as a flex nibble, don't hesitate to include a quarter measure of dark colored rice to round out the SmartCarb serving. On the off chance that you'd rather make it a flex supper, you can eat the two servings. Simply make sure to slice the sauce down the middle so you don't surpass your allocated additional items for the day.

Ingredients

- Coconut Shrimp

- 3 oz. peeled cooked shrimp

- 2 Tbsp. whole wheat flour

- ¼ cup shredded coconut, unsweetened

- ¼ cup panko bread crumbs

- 1 egg, beaten

- Spicy Apricot Sauce

- 2 Tbsp. apricot preserves, sugar-free

- ½ tsp. light soy sauce

- 1 tsp. vinegar

- Pinch red pepper flakes

Guidelines:

- Preheat air fryer at 350 ° F.

- Get ready three dishes: one with flour, one with egg and one with the panko and coconut blended.

- Plunge shrimp into flour, at that point the egg, and afterward the coconut and panko blend.

- Place the covered shrimp into the sear bushel.

- Cook for 5 minutes (cooked shrimp) or 10 minutes (uncooked).

- Meanwhile, consolidate the greater part of the apricot sauce fixings in a little sauce container and mix it over medium warmth until the point when the jam is very much softened. Put aside and present with shrimp.

Apple Dumplings

Ingredients

- 2 very small apples

- 2 tablespoons raisins

- 1 tablespoon brown sugar

- 2 sheets puff pastry

- 2 tablespoons of melted butter

Guidelines

- Preheat your air fryer to 356°F.

- Core and peel the apples. Mix the raisins and the brown sugar.

- Put each apple on one of the puff pastry sheets then fill the core with the raisins and sugar. Fold the pastry around the apple so it is fully covered.

- Place the apple dumplings on a small sheet of foil (so if any juices escape they don't fall into the air fryer). Brush the dough with the melted butter.

- Place in you air fryer and set the timer to 25 minutes and bake the apple dumplings until golden brown and the apples are soft. Turn the apples over one time during cooking so that they will cook evenly.

Air Fried Mozzarella Sticks

A blend of Garlic powder, Italian seasoning, and simply enough Panko breadcrumbs to make the food delightfully firm, will make you select this recipe as your preferred top choice. On the off chance that the 99 calories for each serving still has you in dismay, allows simply say that air fryers are a grimy small abstaining from food mystery. This little, yet capable machine serves up all the wow factor related with a grand plate of mozzarella sticks in an essentially more advantageous way.

Ingredient

- 6 mozzarella string cheese sticks, low fat
- 1 cup Panko breadcrumbs, plain
- 1 large egg
- 1 Tbsp. Italian seasoning
- 1 tsp. garlic powder

Guidelines

- Preheat Air Fryer at 400° F.
- Beat the egg in a little bowl.
- Combine bread scraps, garlic powder and Italian seasoning.

- Plunge string cheddar into the bowl of egg and afterward coat with the breadcrumbs blend. Rehash for outstanding sticks of cheddar.

- Stop the sticks for 20-30 minutes.

- Air fry cheese sticks for 10 minutes, flipping most of the way for cooking.

Philly Chicken Cheesesteak Stromboli

Ingredients

- ½ onions, Piece

- 1 teaspoon vegetable oil

- 2 boneless, skinless chicken bosoms, somewhat solidified and cut thin on the inclination (around 1 pound)

- 1 tablespoon of Worcestershire sauce

- Salt and crisply ground dark pepper

- 14ounces' pizza batter (locally acquired or natively constructed)

- 1½ container ground cheddar

- ½ container Cheese Whiz (or other bumped cheddar sauce), warmed delicately in the microwave

Guidelines

- Pre-warm the air fryer to 400°F.

- Hurl the cut onion with oil and air-fry for 8 minutes, mixing part of the way through the cooking time. Include the cut chicken and Worcestershire sauce to the air fryer basket, and hurl to equally disseminate the ingredients. Season the blend with salt and crisply ground dark pepper and air-broil for 8 minutes, mixing several times amid the cooking procedure. Expel the chicken and onion from the air fryer and let the blend cool a bit.

- On a softly floured surface, roll or press the pizza batter out into a 13-inch by 11-inch rectangle, with the long side nearest to you. Sprinkle half of the cheddar over the batter leaving a vacant 1-inch outskirt from the edge most distant far from you. Top the cheddar with the chicken and onion blend, spreading it out uniformly. Shower the cheddar sauce over the meat and sprinkle the rest of the cheddar to finish everything.

- Begin rolling the Stromboli far from you and toward the vacant fringe. Ensure the filling remains firmly tucked inside the roll. At last, tuck the closures of the batter in and squeeze the crease close. Place the crease side down and shape the Stromboli into a U-shape to fit noticeable all around rotisserie bushel. Cut 4 little openings with the tip of a sharp blade uniformly in the highest point of the batter and softly brush the Stromboli with a little oil.

- Pre-warm the air fryer to 370°F.

- Splash or brush air fryer container with oil and exchange the U-molded Stromboli to the air fryer bushel. Air-fry to transform the Stromboli out of the air fryer basket and after that slide it again into the basket off the plate.)

- To evacuate painstakingly flip Stromboli over onto a cutting board. Allow it to cool for some minutes previously serving. Cut the Stromboli into 3-inch pieces and present with ketchup for plummeting if wanted.

Air Fryer Frittata

Rather than wandering off in fantasy land about the informal breakfast nourishments your friends are getting a charge out of, create a light, protein-pressed and flavorful dinner that'll dispatch your day the correct way. Mushrooms, tomato and chive draw out the serious canons for plant new flavor to supplement feathery billows of egg white that needs no help from cheese.

Ingredients

- 1 cup egg whites

- 2 Tbsp. skim milk

- ¼ cup sliced tomato

- ¼ cup sliced mushrooms

- 2 Tbsp. chopped fresh chives

- Black pepper, to taste

Guidelines

- Preheat Air Fryer at 320° F.

- In a bowl, combine all the ingredients.

- Transfer to a greased frying pan (which may be provided with the air fryer) or to the bottom of the air fryer (after removing the accessory)

- Bake for 15 minutes or until frittata is cooked through

Roasted Vegetable Pasta Salad

This serviette of mixed greens incorporates the finish of summer vegetables yet cooked (or flame broiled first). Why would that be an awesome summer food? Since you can make it early – in reality it needs some time for the flavors to blend - abandoning you allowing something even better, which is, watch another person do the flame broiling!

Ingredients

- 1 orange pepper, huge piece

- 1 green pepper, huge piece

- 1 red pepper, huge piece

- 1 zucchini, cut down through the middle moons

- 1 yellow squash cut down the middle moons

- 1 red onion, piece

- 4 ounces dark colored mushrooms split

- 1 teaspoon Italian flavoring

- Salt and new ground dark pepper

- 1 pound of cooked penne rigatoni,

- 1 container grape tomatoes split

- ½ glasses set Kalamata olives, divided

- 3 tablespoons balsamic vinegar

- ¼ glass olive oil

- 2 tablespoons cleaved crisp basil

Guidelines

- Preheat the air fryer to 380°F.

- Place the peppers, zucchini, yellow squash, red onion and mushrooms in a substantial bowl, sprinkle with a tad bit of the olive oil and hurl to coat well. Include the Italian flavoring and season with salt and pepper. Air-fry for 12 to 14 minutes, until the point that the vegetables are delicate yet not soft. Mix or shake the container part of the way through the cooking time to uniformly broil vegetables.

- Consolidate the cooked pasta, broiled vegetables, tomatoes and olives in a substantial bowl and blend well. Include the balsamic vinegar and hurl. Add enough olive oil to coat everything pleasantly (you may not utilize everything). Season with salt and naturally ground dark pepper to taste.

- Refrigerate the plate of mixed greens until when you are prepared to serve. Mix in the crisp basil just before serving.

CHAPTER 8

DESSERTS AND SWEETS

Onion Rings

This recipe is one of the most effortless, yet most delectable bites to make utilizing an air fryer, all you require is to utilize the air searing method and this formula to get a similar outcome, yet significantly more beneficial.

Ingredients:

- 4 ounces of frozen battered onion rings

- onion rings air fryer recipe

Guidelines

- Add the onion rings into the frying basket of your air fryer.

- Once again, if there is a French fry setting available, choose it, since it delivers the result you want. The onion rings should fry for 10 minutes.

- After 10 minutes, remove the basket and toss the onion rings.

- Return it into the air fryer and repeat the cooking process for another 10 minutes.

- If you feel they aren't ready yet, you can cook them longer.

- Serve them with any preferred sauce

Air Baked Molten Lava Cakes

Ingredients

- 1.5 TBS Self-rising Flour

- 3.5 TBS Baker's Sugar (Not Powdered)

- 3.5 OZ Unsalted Butter

- 3.5 OZ Dark Chocolate (Pieces or Chopped)

- 2 Eggs

Guidelines

- Preheat Your Air Fryer to 375F

- Grease and flour 4 standard oven safe ramekins.

- Melt dark chocolate and butter in a microwave safe bowl on level 7 for 3 minutes, stirring throughout. Remove from microwave and stir until even consistency.

- Whisk/Beat the eggs and sugar until pale and frothy.

- Pour melted chocolate mixture into egg mixture. Stir in flour. Use a spatula to combine everything evenly.

- Fill the ramekins about 3/4 full with cake mixture and bake in preheated air fryer at 375F for 10 minutes.

- Remove from the air fryer and allow to cool in ramekin for 2 minutes. Carefully turn ramekins upside down onto serving plate, tapping the bottom with a butter knife to loosen edges.

- Cake should release from ramekin with little effort and center should appear dark/gooey. Enjoy warm a-la-mode or with a raspberry drizzle.

Apple Fries with Caramel Cream Dip

This is one delicious treat you'll get out of your air-fryer. The apples get warm and only somewhat delicate and delicate within, yet can hold there possess when you plunge them. You can likewise have a go at plunging into chocolate sauce or simply caramel sauce on the off chance that you need to keep it dairy free.

Ingredients

- 3 Pink Lady or Honey-crisp apples, peeled, cored and cut into 8 wedges

- ½ container flour

- 3 eggs, beaten

- 1 container graham wafer scraps

- ¼ container sugar

- 8 ounces whipped cream cheddar

- ½ container caramel sauce, in addition to additional for embellish

Guidelines

- Hurl the apple cuts and flour together in a substantial bowl. Set up a digging station by putting the beaten eggs in a single shallow dish, and consolidating the pounded graham wafers and sugar in a moment shallow dish. Plunge every apple cut into the egg, and after that into the graham saltine morsels. Coat the cuts on all sides and place the covered cuts on a treat sheet.

- Pre-warm the air fryer to 380°F. Shower or brush the base of the air fryer bushel with oil.

- Air-fry the apples in bunches. Place one layer of apple cuts noticeable all around fryer crate and shower delicately with oil. Air-fry for 4 minutes. Turn the apples over and air - fry for an extra 2 minutes.

- While apples are cooking influence caramel cream to plunge. Consolidate the whipped cream cheddar and caramel sauce, blending great. Exchange the Caramel Cream Dip into a serving dish and sprinkle extra caramel sauce over the best.

- Serve the apple fries hot with the caramel cream plunge as an afterthought!

Air fryer Caramel Cheesecake

These are nearly nothing and charming and ideal for the Airfryer and they are simple to make.

Ingredients

- Hand Mixer

- Spring Form Pan

- Instant Pot

- 6 Digestives

- 50 g Melted Butter

- 1 Can Condensed Milk

- 500 g Soft Cheese

- 250 g Caster Sugar

- 4 Large Eggs

- 1 Tbsp Vanilla Essence

- 1 Tbsp Melted Chocolate

Guidelines

- In your Instant Pot place the can of condensed milk in it without its can wrappings submerged in water. Cook it for 40 minutes on manual and remember to seal it.

- Preheat the Airfryer to 180c.

- Flour the sides and bottom of your spring form pan with your hands so that it becomes non-stick.

- Crumble the digestive biscuits by giving it a hammering with a rolling pin inside a sandwich bag or inside its wrappers.

- Mix the melted butter into the crumbled digestives inside the spring form pan (less washing up that way) and using your hands make sure it pushes down on the bottom.

- In a mixing bowl and using a hand mixer, mix the sugar into the soft cheese until it is nice and fluffy. Add the eggs and vanilla essence and mix in with the mixer. Put to one side.

- When the condensed milk is done and cooled down, open it up and pour the caramel into the bowl. Mix it in with a fork and then place the mixture into the spring form pan over the biscuit base.

- Level it and make it smooth with the spatula.

- Cook for 15 minutes at 180c, 10 minutes at 160c and then a last 15 minutes at 150c.

- When it is done, place it in the fridge to cool for 6 hours.

- Drizzle over the top with fork small amounts of melted chocolate and leftover caramel when done.

Air Fried Sugared Dough Dippers with Chocolate Amaretto Sauce

It has never been this easy! If you have purchase bread or pizza batter, you should simply roll and air fry!

Ingredients

- 1 pound of bread batter, defrosted

- ½ dissolved cup spread butter

- ¾ to 1 container of sugar

- 1 container overwhelming cream

- 12ounces of quality semi-sweet chocolate chips

- 2 tablespoons Amaretto alcohol (or almond extricate)

Guidelines

- Roll the batter into 214-inch logs. Cut each sign into 20 cuts. Cut each cut down the middle and bend the batter parts together 3 to 4 times. Place the contorted batter on a treat sheet, brush with softened margarine and sprinkle sugar over the mixture turns.

- Pre-warm the air fryer to 340°F.

- Brush the base of the air fryer crate with liquefied spread. Air-fry the mixture winds in bunches. Place 8 to 12 (contingent upon the span of your air fryer) noticeable all around fryer basket.

- Air-fry for 4 minutes. Turn the mixture strips over and brush the opposite favor margarine. Air-fry for an extra 3 minutes.

- While batter is cooking, influence the chocolate amaretto to sauce. Convey the overwhelming cream to a stew over medium warmth. Place the chocolate contributes an expansive bowl and pour the hot cream over the chocolate chips. Blend until the point that the chocolate begins to liquefy. At that point change to a wire whisk and race until the point when the chocolate is totally liquefied and the sauce is smooth. Blend in the Amaretto. Exchange to a serving dish.

- As the clusters of batter turns are finished, put them into a shallow dish. Brush with softened margarine and liberally coat with sugar, shaking the dish to cover the 2 sides.

- Serve the sugared mixture scoops with the warm chocolate Amaretto sauce as an addendum.

Crispy Fried Spring Rolls

The disparitiesin hot air fryer recipes are quite much, but this recipe in adapts to the air frying technique

Ingredients

- 120g cooked chicken breast
- 1 celery stalk
- 30 g carrot
- 30 g mushrooms
- ½ tsp finely chopped ginger
- 1 tsp sugar
- 1 tsp chicken stock powder
- 1 egg
- 1 tsp corn starch
- 8 spring roll wrappers

Guidelines

- Tear the cooked chicken breasts into shreds. Slice the celery, carrot and mushroom into long thin strips.

- Place the shredded chicken into a bowl and mix with the celery, carrot and mushroom. Add the ginger, sugar and chicken stock powder and stir evenly to make the spring roll filling.

- Whisk the egg, and then add the corn starch and mix to create a thick paste. Set aside.

- Place some filling onto each spring roll wrapper and roll it up, then seal the ends with the egg mixture. For a crispy result, lightly brush the spring rolls with oil.

- Preheat the Airfryer to 200°C.

- Place the rolls into the Airfryer basket and slide the basket into the Airfryer. Set the timer for 4 minutes. Serve with sweet chill sauce

Midnight Nutella Banana Sandwich

These debauched basic treats are an immaculate midnight nibble and are particularly great with a little nip of Grand Marnier. You can make numerous minor departure from this sandwich by substituting different elements for the bananas – attempt raspberries, strawberries or even cuts of ready peach.

Ingredients

- Mollified Butter,

- 4 pieces of white bread

- ¼ container chocolate hazelnut spread (Nutella®)

- 1 banana

Guidelines

- Pre-warm the air fryer to 370°F.

- Spread the mollified margarine on 1 side of the considerable number of cuts of bread and place the cuts, buttered side down on the counter. Spread the chocolate hazelnut spread on the opposite side of the bread cuts. Cut the banana down the middle and after that cut every half into 3 cuts the long way. Place the banana cuts on 2 cuts of bread and best with the rest of the cuts of bread to make 2 sandwiches. Cut the sandwiches down the middle (triangles or rectangles) – this will help them all fit noticeable all around fryer on the double. Exchange the sandwiches to the air fryer.

- Air-fry at 370°F for 4 minutes. Flip the sandwiches over and air-broil for another 2 to 3 minutes or until the point when the best bread cuts are pleasantly cooked. Present yourself with a glass of drain or a midnight nightcap while the sandwiches cool and then enjoy!

Blueberry Cheesecake

This particular one is stunning in light of the fact that you can enrich it as you wish and after that take it to a birthday party, a dedicating, a child shower or for a cookout on the shoreline

Ingredients

- Spring Form Pan

- 6 Digestives

- 50 g Melted Butter

- 600 g Soft Cheese

- 300 g Caster Sugar

- 4 Large Eggs

- 100 g Fresh Blueberries

- 2 Tbsp Greek Yoghurt

- 1 Tbsp Vanilla Essence

- 5 Tbsp Icing Sugar

Guidelines

- Preheat your Airfryer to 180c.

- Flour the sides and bottom of your spring form pan so that when you cook your cheesecake that it won't stick.

- Crumble the digestive biscuits and mix them with the melted butter. Push them down into the bottom of the spring form pan so that they form the base.

- Cream the cheese and the sugar together with a hand mixer until they are light but incredibly thick and fluffy.

- Add the eggs (one at a time), the Greek Yoghurt, vanilla essence and mix everything as you put it in.

- Chop the blueberries into quarters. Place a quarter of them into the soft cheese mixture and mix well.

- Using a big spoon (I used a soup spoon) spoon the mixture into the spring form pan and use a spatula to flatten any bubbles and to give it a very smooth feeling.

- Place in the Airfryer and cook at 180c for 15 minutes, 160c for 10 minutes and then a further 15 minutes at 150c. This will ensure that it cooked everywhere and not just on the top.

- When the Airfryer beeps, place it into the fridge and allow cooling for 12 hours.

- Once cooled take the rest of the blueberries and cook them in a pan with a little icing sugar and once they are melted down to half their size, spoon over the cheesecake for the top layer.

- Serve.

Birthday Cake Cheesecake

Add some crisp blueberries to your cheesecake and you can have a delightful summer cheesecake. It doesn't require as long in the cooler to set.

Ingredients

- Airfryer
- Hand Mixer
- Spring Form Pan
- 6 Digestives
- 50 g Melted Butter
- 800 g Soft Cheese
- 500 g Caster Sugar
- 4 Tbsp Cocoa Powder
- 6 Large Eggs
- 2 Tbsp Honey
- 1 Tbsp Vanilla Essence
- Melted Chocolate

Guidelines

- Flour the bottom and sides of a spring form pan so that it no longer sticks.

- Bash your digestive biscuits inside a sandwich bag with a rolling pin until they resemble breadcrumbs. Mix into them the melted butter and then push them down into the bottom of your spring form pan.

- In a mixing bowl mix together the soft cheese and caster sugar with a hand mix. Add to it 5 out of 6 of the eggs, honey and vanilla essence and mix with the hand mixer until everything is well mixed in.

- Using a large spoon, spoon half of it into the spring form pan over the crumbly base. Pat it down with a spatula and get rid of any lumps and bumps. Place the rest of the mixture into the fridge.

- Cook it at 180c for 20 minutes, 15 minutes at 160c and then a final 20 minutes at 150c. Transfer it to the fridge and allow to set for a further hour.

- After an hour, get the rest of the mixture out of the fridge. Crack in the final egg and the cocoa powder and give it a good mix with a fork.

- Spoon it over the set bottom cheesecake layer and return to the fridge for 11 hours.

- After it has been resting decorate it as you please. Splash melted chocolate over the sides, add lots of chocolate pieces or however you see fit depending on the occasion.

- Serve.

Fried Hot Prawns with Cocktail Sauce

Ingredients:

- 8-12 fresh king prawns

- 1 tbsp of cider or wine vinegar

- 3 tbsp of mayonnaise

- 1 tbsp of ketchup

- 1 tsp chili flakes

- 1/2 tsp of sea salt

- 1/2 tsp of freshly ground black pepper

- 1 tsp of chili powder

Guidelines

- Preheat your air fryer to 180°C.

- To season the prawns, mix all the spices in a bowl.

- After doing so, add the prawns and mix them well with all the seasonings.

- Once seasoned, the prawns are ready for frying.

- Place the prawns into the frying basket, and return the basket into the air fryer.

- These prawns should be cooked for 6 to 8 minutes, so adjust the timer accordingly. The frying time depends on the size of the prawns.

- The remaining ingredients from the list should be used for the cocktail sauce.

- Mix them together and serve the fried prawns with it.

- After you taste this dish, it will definitely be among the best air fryer recipes for you

CHAPTER 9

SOUP

Asian Shrimp Noodle Soup

Ingredients

- 24 vast shrimp, unpeeled

- 4 mugs vegetable stock

- 1 tablespoon of vegetable oil

- 1 red onion, cut

- 2 carrots, cut into julienne strips

- 2 ribs celery, cut on the inclination ¼" thick

- 2minced cloves garlic,

- 2 tablespoons ground crisp ginger

- ½ - 1 red bean stew pepper, divided

- 2 (14-ounce) jars coconut drain

- ½ pound rice vermicelli noodles

- 1 tablespoon of soy sauce

- 3pieces of scallions,

- ¼ glass new cilantro clears out

- 1 lime, cut into chunks

Guidelines

- Peel and devein the shrimp, holding the shells. Put the peeled shrimp aside. Consolidate the vegetable stock and held shrimp shells in a pot. Stew together for 30 minutes. At that point strain out and dispose of the shrimp shells, saving the capital.

- Heat a stockpot or Dutch oven over medium warmth. Include the vegetable oil and daintily sauté the onion, carrot, and celery until delicate – around 6 to 8 minutes. Include the garlic, ginger, bean stew pepper parts and cook for 1 to 2 minutes. Include the saved vegetable stock and coconut drain, and convey to a stew. Stew for 20 minutes.

- In the meantime, in a different bowl or pot, pour bubbling water over the rice noodles and let them sit while the soup stews.

- Deplete and add the noodles to the soup, alongside the shrimp, soy sauce,and scallions. Stew just until the point when the shrimp is pink and obscure – around 2 to 4 minutes. Include the cilantro and present with the lime wedges.

Basic Chicken Noodle Soup

Hardly is any other thing are as improving as a bowl of chicken noodle soup. This fundamental form never neglects to fulfill and is significantly less demanding to make than you might suspect

Ingredients

- 1 tablespoon olive oil

- 1 onion, finely chopped

- 2finely slashed carrots,

- 2 ribs celery finely cut

- 2 cloves garlic, finely slashed

- ½ teaspoon dried thyme

- 1 inlet leaf

- 2 quarts' great quality or hand-crafted chicken or vegetable stock

- 3 containers cooked chicken, destroyed or cut into chomp estimated pieces

- 1½ mugsextensive egg noodles salt, to taste newly ground dark pepper

- ¼ container hacked new parsley

Guidelines

- Heat a stockpot or Dutch stove over medium fire. Include the olive oil and delicately sauté the onion, carrot, and celery until delicate – around 6 to 8 minutes.

- Include the garlic, thyme and inlet leaf and cook for one more minute.

- Include the chicken stock, and convey to a stew. Stew for 20 minutes.

- Include the cooked chicken and noodles in the pot and cook until the point when noodles are still somewhat firm – 6 to 8 minutes.

- Purge the straight leaf from the soup, season with salt and pepper, include parsley and serve quickly

Curried Sweet Potato Soup

Ingredients

- 2 tablespoons of butter

- 1 tablespoon olive oil

- ½ onion, hacked (about ½ glass)

- 4 to 6 sweet potatoes, peeled and diced

- 1 tablespoon of curry powder

- 4 containers chicken stock, vegetable stock or water

- ¾ container squeezed orange

- ½ teaspoon salt or more to taste newly ground dark pepper

- ½ container harsh cream (discretionary)

- 3 tablespoons of hacked crisp parsley

Guidelines

- Dissolve the margarine alongside the olive oil in a stockpot or Dutch stove over medium warmth.

- Include the onion and cook for 4 to 7 minutes. The onion ought to be translucent, not darker.

- Include the sweet potatoes and curry powder, and keep on cooking for another 6 to 8 minutes.

- Include the chicken stock, vegetable stock or water and keep on simmering for an additional 20 minutes. Mix in the squeezed orange.

- Utilizing a blender, sustenance processor, nourishment factory or inundation blender, puree the soup until the point that no knots remain and the soup is smooth.

- Restore the soup to the stovetop and thin the soup with water until you've achieved the coveted consistency.

- Include salt and naturally ground dark pepper.

- Present with a bit of sour cream and cleaved parsley to embellish.

Tuscan Chicken and White Bean Soup

This soup is flavorful and simple to make. It will warm and top you off!

Ingredients

- 4ounces' pancetta (or bacon on the off chance that you can't discover pancetta)

- 1 onion, finely diced

- 3minced cloves garlic,

- 1 teaspoon dried thyme

- 1 teaspoon dried basil

- ½ teaspoon dried rosemary

- 2 tablespoons tomato glue

- 3 containers chicken stock

- 1 (28-ounce) tomatoes

- 2 glasses destroyed, cooked chicken

- 2 (14-ounce) jars white cannellini beans, depleted and flushed

- 4 pieces ciabatta rolls or 1 ciabatta baguette,

- Olive oil

- 4 ounces crisp infant spinach, cleaned

- 1 teaspoon salt

- Naturally ground dark pepper

- Square of Parmesan cheese

Guidelines

- Place pancetta in an expansive stockpot and cook until the point when a portion of the fat has been rendered out – around 6 to 8 minutes.

- Expel the pancetta with an opened spoon and put it aside.

- Add the onion to the stockpot and cook until the point when the onion begins to relax – around 6 minutes.

- Include the garlic, thyme, basil, rosemary and tomato glue, mix to mix well, and cook for one more moment or 2. Include the chicken stock, tomatoes, destroyed chicken and beans to the pot and blend well.

- Stew the soup for 30 minutes. While the soup is stewing, pre-warm a skillet over medium warmth.

- Include olive oil and toast the cut side of the ciabatta rolls or cuts in the skillet until pleasantly cooked.

- Exorcize the soup from the excess heat and mix in the spinach. Season to taste with salt and pepper.

- Serve the soup with a portion of the cooked pancetta sprinkled to finish everything, a few shards of

Parmesan cheddar (made by peeling the cheddar with a potato peeler) and the toasted ciabatta bread.

SOUS VIDE COOKBOOK

*Step By Step Guide And Proven Recipes
For Sous Vide Meals*

John Carter

The information herein is offered for informational purposes solely, and is universal as so. The presentation of the information is without contract or any type of guarantee assurance.

The trademarks that are used are without any consent, and the publication of the trademark is without permission or backing by the trademark owner. All trademarks and brands within this book are for clarifying purposes only and are the owned by the owners themselves, not affiliated with this document.

TABLE OF CONTENTS

INTRODUCTION 258

CHAPTER ONE 259

    WHAT IS SOUS VIDE COOKING? 259

CHAPTER TWO 266

    SOUS VIDE HONEY-ROSEMARY LAMB SHANK 266

CHAPTER THREE 269

    SOUS VIDE BEER-BRAISED PORK SHANK 269

CHAPTER FOUR 272

    SOUS VIDE LAMB STEW 272

CHAPTER FIVE 274

    SOUS VIDE LEMON AND BLUEBERRY 274

CHAPTER SIX 276

    SOUS VIDE CHICKEN 276

CHAPTER SEVEN 279

    72 HOURS SOUS VIDE BBQ SHORT RIBS 279

CHAPTER EIGHT 281

    TAIWANESE CORN ON THE COB 281

CHAPTER NINE 283

    SOUS VIDE CHUCK-EYE STEAK DIANE 283

CHAPTER TEN 286

OVERNIGHT OATMEAL WITH STEWED FRUIT
COMPOTE 286

CHAPTER ELEVEN 288

ORANGE ROSEMARY INFUSED VINEGAR 288

CHAPTER TWELVE 289

BLACKBERRY BASIL INFUSED VINEGAR 289

CHAPTER THIRTEEN 290

CARROT AND DAIKON QUICK PICKLE.................... 290

CHAPTER FOURTEEN 292

CHOCOLATE ZABAGLIONE 292

CHAPTER FIFTEEN... 294

VANILLA BEAN ICE CREAM 294

CHAPTER SIXTEEN 296

SOUS VIDE CORNED BEEF AND CABBAGE............. 296

CHAPTER SEVENTEEN 298

SOUS VIDE BROWN BUTTER SCALLOPS................ 298

CHAPTER EIGHTEEN 300

SOUS-VIDE CHAR SIU 300

CHAPTER NINETEEN 303

SOUS VIDE SESAME SALMON WITH SOBA
NOODLES 303

CHAPTER TWENTY 306

    PORK TENDERLOIN WITH ROSEMARY GARLIC
    MAPLE GLAZE 306

CHAPTER TWENTY ONE 308

    SOUS VIDE CHEESECAKE 308

CHAPTER TWENTY TWO 310

    SOUS VIDE BONELESS PORK CHOP 310

CHAPTER TWENTY THREE................................312

    SOUS VIDE SHORT RIBS 312

CHAPTER TWENTY FOUR 314

    SOUS VIDE SAUSAGE 314

CHAPTER TWENTY FIVE...................................316

    SOUS VIDE HALIBUT..................................316

CHAPTER TWENTY SIX 318

    SOUS VIDE POACHED EGGS + AVOCADO TOAST... 318

CHAPTER TWENTY SEVEN 320

    SOUS VIDE COD...320

CHAPTER TWENTY EIGHT.................................322

    SOUS VIDE COLD BREW COFFEE 322

CHAPTER TWENTY NINE 324

    SOUS VIDE GARLIC HERB BUTTER STEAK............324

CHAPTER THIRTY 326

    SOUS VIDE CARROTS 326

CHAPTER THIRTY ONE 327

    SOUS VIDE LAMB CHOPS WITH BASIL
    CHIMICHURRI 327

CHAPTER THIRTY TWO 329

    SOUS VIDE DUCK LEGS 329

CHAPTER THIRTY THREE 331

    SOUS VIDE SPICED AUBERGINE WITH
    TURMERIC AND COCONUT SAUCE, CASHEW
    BUTTER AND CRISPY KALE 331

CHAPTER THIRTY FOUR 334

    SOUS VIDE BRUSSELS SPROUTS AND SPROUT
    TOPS, MISO BUTTER, CASHEW 334

CHAPTER THIRTY FIVE 336

    SOUS VIDE LEEKS 336

CHAPTER THIRTY SIX 338

    POLENTA SOUS VIDE 338

CHAPTER THIRTY SEVEN 339

    SOUS VIDE FENNEL AND ORANGE QUINOA
    SALAD 339

CHAPTER THIRTY EIGHT 342

    BEETROOT WITH PICKLED QUINCE 342

CHAPTER THIRTY NINE..345

   SOUS VIDE POTATO RÖSTI..345

CHAPTER FORTY 347

   PUMPKIN VELOUTÉ WITH WILD MUSHROOMS ... 347

CHAPTER FORTY ONE 349

   PICKLED RADISH, DILL EMULSION AND
   PUFFED QUINOA 349

CHAPTER FORTY TWO 352

   SOUS VIDE PIGS EARS..352

CHAPTER FORTY THREE 354

   SUCKLING PIG WITH CHOU FARCI, HUMMUS
   AND CHICKPEA FRICASSEE 354

CHAPTER FORTY FOUR..362

   SOUS VIDE PORK BELLY 362

CHAPTER FORTY FIVE 364

   PORK SHOULDER WITH HISPI CABBAGE AND
   APPLES 364

CHAPTER FORTY SIX..369

   TEQUILA CHICKEN...369

CHAPTER FORTY SEVEN...371

   SOUS VIDE CHICKEN WITH ENGLISH MUSTARD
   AND BROAD BEANS..371

CHAPTER FORTY EIGHT..374

    SOUS VIDE MACKEREL 374

CHAPTER FORTY NINE 376

    SOUS VIDE SEA BASS 376

CHAPTER FIFTY 378

    SOUS VIDE BEEF AND PRUNE TAGINE....................378

CHAPTER FIFTY ONE 381

    SPICED PINEAPPLE WITH WHIPPED CREAM
    CHEESE YOGHURT AND GINGER BISCUITS 381

INTRODUCTION

So you are all ready to try sous vide for yourself, but are at a loss of where to start? Or you have already begun your sous vide exploration and are ready to elevate your recipes to the next level?

Either way, we've got the cookbook for you. Sous vide is a fairly simple method of cooking that employs submersion of sealed bags of food in water that is held at a specific temperature for a precise amount of time. This is done to cook the food perfectly at the desired level of doneness. You can cook the same thing over and over again with the same delicious results knowing it will be good each time.

Getting started with sous vide cooking can be a bit daunting for those without experience, even though this revolutionary method of cooking is easy to learn. It's important for beginners to read up on the sous vide process in order to obtain the best performance from your device and to ensure safety. On the other hand, even those who are experienced with sous vide can learn incredible tips and new mouthwatering recipes to add to their own sous vide cooking arsenal. While I do encourage sous vide enthusiasts to research information online, having a sous vide cookbook in your kitchen is an absolute must – especially for the quick and easy sous vide time and temperature chart.

CHAPTER ONE

WHAT IS SOUS VIDE COOKING?

Once limited to the pros, sous vide (pronounced sue-veed) is a cooking method that uses specific temperature control to deliver consistent, restaurant-quality results. High-end restaurants have been making use of sous vide cooking for ages to prepare food to the exact level of doneness desired, every time. The method recently became famous for home cooks with the availability of reasonably priced and easy-to-use sous vide precision cooking equipments.

Sous vide, which means "under vacuum" in French, is the process of vacuum-sealing food in a bag, then cooking it to a very precise temperature inside a water bath. This method produces results that are cannot be achieved through any other method of cooking.

Sous vide cooking is a lot easier than you might think, and typically involves three simple steps:

1. Affix your precision cooker to a pot of water and set the time and temperature according to the level of doneness you desire.

2. Put your food inside a sealable bag and clip it to the side of the pot.

3. Finish up by searing, grilling, or broiling the food to put in a crispy, golden exterior layer.

Why should I cook sous vide?

Sous vide cooking makes use of precise temperature control with circulation to produce results that you can't achieve with any other cooking method. The reason is when using the conventional methods of cooking, you don't have power over heat and temperature. As a result, it's very hard and time consuming to consistently cook good food. Food ends up overcooked on the outside, with only a small portion in the center that is cooked to the temperature you desire. Food loses its flavor, overcooks easily, and ends up with a dry, chewy texture.

With precise temperature control in the kitchen, sous vide gives the following benefits:

Consistency

Since you cook your food to a specific temperature for a precise amount of time, you can look forward to very consistent results.

Taste

Food cooks in its juices. This makes sure that the food is moist, juicy and tender.

Waste reduction

Traditionally prepared food dries out and leads to waste. For instance, on average, conventionally cooked steak loses up to 40% of its volume due to drying out. Steak cooked through precision cooking, loses none of its volume.

Flexibility

Traditional cooking can necessitate your regular attention. Precision cooking brings food to an precise temperature and holds it. There is no need to be anxious about overcooking.

How are sous vide results better?

Sous vide supplies down-to-the-degree control in the kitchen to deliver the most tender, flavorful food you've ever had. With this, it is super simple to get restaurant-quality results from edge to edge.

What equipment do I need to cook sous vide?

It's actually very cheap and easy to get started with sous vide cooking thanks to the recent availability of sous vide equipments created for the home cook. You'll need a few things:

- A sous vide precision cooking device

- Packaging for your food, like resealable bags or canning jars

- A container to hold the water

Types of Sous Vide Machines

Sous vide equipment has been in existence for decades in professional kitchens all over the world, but it has always been huge, expensive, and overloaded with multifaceted features. This type of equipment finally made its way into high-end specialty retail shops, but remained restricted to chefs and consumers with broad culinary experience.

Cooking shows, social media, and online communities have furthered consumers' knowledge of sous vide cooking, and now sous vide has become accessible to home cooks. There are now lots of sous vide options available to the home cook.

Below are a few types of devices for you to consider when you're ready to create your ultimate sous vide setup:

Sous Vide Immersion Circulator

The Immersion circulator heats water and circulates it around the pot to maintain precise temperatures evenly. Immersion circulators are a cheap and an easy-to-use sous vide machine option. They do not come with a built-in water bath, so they take up very little space in your kitchen. The immersion circulator sous vide devices don't need additional equipment to get started because they clamp on and alter to any pot you already have.

Sous Vide Water Oven

Water ovens are usually referred to as countertop water baths. They are fully-contained, sous vide devices that are about the size of a microwave and normally cost $500+. Sous vide water ovens heat water, but unlike immersion circulators, they do not circulate the water. This can lead to irregularity in the food's resulting texture. Examples of water ovens include SousVide Supreme, AquaChef, and Gourmia. Multi-use cookers like Oliso, Gourmia and Instant Pot also offer sous vide appliances.

DIY Sous Vide Hacks

Cooler, rice cooker, and slow cooker hacks are good options for exploring sous vide cooking before you decide to buy a device. The Food Lab's J. Kenji Lopez-Alt has a great post on sous vide beer cooler hacks.

Sous Vide Packaging

Sealing foods prevents evaporation and allows for the most efficient transfer energy from the water to the food. To do so, simply place your seasoned food in a plastic bag and release the air using the water immersion method, a straw, or a vacuum sealer.

You don't need a vacuum sealer to cook sous vide. There are lots of options, here are a few of the best types of sous vide packaging:

Sous Vide Containers

Containers clip onto the side of any pot or vessel with an adjustable clamp. So, you can use any size of pot that you already have at home. If you're planning to cook a lot of food at once, plastic bins like Cambro and Rubbermaid are great choices.

You can also explore creating a dedicated sous vide cooking vessel.

Resealable Bags or Jars

Resealable bags are very resourceful, and can be used with the water immersion method to eliminate air from the bag. We suggest heavy-duty, BPA-free bags, like Ziplock's freezer bags.

Reusable Silicone Bags

Reusable sous vide bags made from silicone, like these Stasher Reusable Silicone Sous Vide Bag bags; make it easy to enjoy the same quality results night after night.

Vacuum Sealing Bags

You don't need to buy a vacuum sealer and vacuum seal bags, but they work great for batch cooking. Foodsaver and Oliso are good options, and both are pretty inexpensive.

Canning Jars

Numerous different types of foods can also be cooked in glass canning jars. Beans and grains both cook well in jars, as do desserts such as cakes and custards.

How do I get set up for my first sous vide cook?

Getting set up with your first sous vide cook is easy:

1. Simply clip the Sous Vide Precision Cooker to a pot or container and fill with water above the minimum fill line.

2. Season your food and put it in the bag. Put the bag in the water bath and clip it to the side of the pot.

3. Choose what you're cooking from our compilation of recipes and sous vide guides, then press start on the screen of your cooker.

CHAPTER TWO

SOUS VIDE HONEY-ROSEMARY LAMB SHANK

We love lamb in all its gamey glory, but not everybody feels the same way. Nevertheless, with this big flavorful recipe for honey-rosemary lamb shank, we've been able to change a few lamb-fearing hearts and minds.

After 48 hours with Sous Vide Precision Cooker, the meat is fall-off-the-bone soft and the vegetables deeply seasoned. A fast reduction of the cooking liquid finishes the vegetables to perfection and makes a rich, aromatic, and perfectly sweet sauce that balances the often-bold taste of lamb.

Ingredients for 4

- 4 lamb shanks

- 2 tablespoons olive oil

- 2 cups all-purpose flour for dusting

- 1 medium yellow onion, peeled and thinly sliced

- 4 garlic cloves, peeled and smashed

- 4 medium carrots, medium dice

- 4 stalks celery, medium dice

- 3 tablespoons tomato paste

- 1/2 cup sherry wine vinegar

- 1 cup red wine

- 3/4 cup honey

- 1 quart beef stock

- 4 sprigs fresh rosemary

- 2 dried bay leaves

- Kosher salt and freshly ground black pepper

How to prepare

- Set your Sous Vide Precision Cooker to 155°F (68.3°C).

- In a big cast-iron skillet, heat oil over high heat until just starting to smoke. Season shanks richly with salt, dust with flour, and sear to golden brown on all sides.

- Take out shanks and set aside. Reduce heat to medium-high and add onion, garlic, carrots, and celery. Season with salt and pepper and cook for 10 minutes. Add in tomato paste and cook for one minute.

- Add in vinegar, wine, honey, stock, rosemary, and bay leaves and cook for two minutes.

- Add in vegetables, sauce, and lamb shanks to vacuum or Ziploc plastic bag, seal, and cook for 48 hours.

- Take out shanks from bag and pat dry, reserving cooking liquid. Place shanks on roasting rack and broil until skin is golden brown, about five minutes. (Watch carefully to make sure it doesn't burn.)

- Add in cooking liquid and vegetables to large saucepan and simmer over medium-high heat until vegetables are tender and sauce is minimized by two-thirds, about 10 minutes.

- Remove shanks from oven, sauce, and serve. For smaller portions, pull the meat from the shank in large chunks and serve with sauce.

CHAPTER THREE

SOUS VIDE BEER-BRAISED PORK SHANK

Ingredients for 4

- 4 pork shanks

- 2 tablespoons extra-virgin olive oil

- 2 cups all-purpose flour for dusting

- 1 medium yellow onion, peeled and thinly sliced

- 4 garlic cloves, peeled and smashed

- 4 medium carrots, medium dice

- 4 stalks celery, medium dice

- 2 tablespoons tomato paste

- 24 ounces of your favorite full-flavored beer (e.g. porter, stout, ale)

- 2 tablespoons soy sauce

- 2 tablespoons honey

- 1 quart pork stock (or chicken or beef)

- 4 sprigs fresh thyme

- 4 sprigs fresh rosemary

- 2 bay leaves

- Kosher salt and freshly ground black pepper

How to prepare

- Set Anova Sous Vide Precision Cooker to 155°F (68.3°C).

- In a large cast-iron skillet, heat oil over high heat until just starting to smoke. Season shanks richly with salt, dust with flour, and sear to golden brown on all sides.

- Take out shanks and set aside. Minimize heat to medium-high and add onion, garlic, carrots, and celery. Season with salt and pepper and cook for 10 minutes. Add tomato paste and cook for one minute.

- Add in beer, soy sauce, honey, stock, thyme, rosemary, and bay leaves and cook for two minutes.

- Add in vegetables, sauce, and pork shanks to vacuum or Ziploc plastic bag, seal, and cook for 48 hours.

- Remove shanks from bag and pat dry, reserving cooking liquid. Place shanks on roasting rack and broil until skin is golden brown, about five minutes. (Watch carefully to make sure they don't burn.)

- Add in cooking liquid and vegetables to large saucepan and simmer over medium-high heat until vegetables are tender and sauce reduced by two-thirds, about 10 minutes.

- Remove shanks from oven, sauce, and serve. For smaller portions, pull the meat from the shank in large chunks and serve with sauce.

CHAPTER FOUR

SOUS VIDE LAMB STEW

Ingredients for 6

- 2 pounds boneless lamb shoulder, cut into 1-inch cubes

- 4 ounces thick-cut bacon, cut into ½ strips

- 1 cup red wine

- 2 tablespoons tomato paste

- 1 quart beef stock

- 4 large shallots, quartered

- 4 medium carrots, peeled and cut into 1-inch pieces

- 4 stalks of celery, cut into 1-inch pieces

- 3 garlic cloves, peeled and smashed

- 1 pound small fingerling potatoes (or small red), cut in half lengthwise

- 4 ounces dried shiitake mushrooms (optional)

- 3 sprigs fresh rosemary

- 3 sprigs fresh thyme

- 2 dried whole bay leaves

- Kosher salt and freshly ground black pepper

How to prepare

- Set the Sous Vide Precision Cooker to 145°F (62.7°C).

- Heat a big cast-iron skillet over medium-high heat. Render bacon until it is golden brown and set aside.

- Season the lamb evenly with salt and pepper and sear in bacon fat until it is golden brown on all sides. (You will likely have to work in several batches.)

- Set lamb to another side and deglaze pan with wine and stock. Add in wine-stock combination, bacon, lamb, any accumulated searing juices, vegetables, and herbs to a large Ziplock or vacuum bag. Seal the bag and cook it for 24 hours.

- Pour the contents of the bag into a big saucepan, removing the pieces of lamb to a plate. (This makes sure the meat doesn't get overcooked or tough while the sauce and vegetables simmer.) Simmer over medium heat until the vegetables are tender and the sauce reduced by half, about 15 minutes.

- Remove the saucepan from the heat, take out the lamb to the pan to warm in the sauce, and serve.

CHAPTER FIVE

SOUS VIDE LEMON AND BLUEBERRY

Crème brûlée is a crowd-pleasing standard French dessert. It can be prepared without stress ahead of time and stored in the refrigerator then quickly finished at the dinner table, making it a great option for a dinner party dessert.

Ingredients for 6

- 6 large egg yolks

- 1 1/3 cups superfine sugar, plus more for sprinkling

- 3 cups heavy (whipping) cream

- Zest of 2 lemons

- 4 tablespoons freshly squeezed lemon juice

- 1 teaspoon vanilla extract

- 1 cup fresh blueberries

How to prepare

- Set your Sous Vide Precision Cooker to 195°F (90.5°C).

- With an electric mixer, whisk together the egg yolks and sugar in a large bowl until it is pale and creamy. Set it aside.

- Pour the cream into a medium saucepan over medium heat and heat to just below boiling point. Be cautious not to burn the cream. Add in the lemon zest, lemon juice, and vanilla into the cream, stirring as you add the lemon juice to evade curdling. Simmer over low heat for 4 to 5 minutes.

- Take out the cream mixture from the heat and cool for 2 to 3 minutes. When cooled, pour a small amount into the egg mixture and whisk to combine. (This tempers the egg mixture so it doesn't scramble when you pour in the rest of the hot cream concoction.) Pour the remaining of the cream mixture into the eggs and stir to mix.

- Divide the blueberries equally among six mini mason jars then pour the egg-cream mixture over the blueberries, dividing equally among the jars.

- Screw on the jar lids to fingertip tightness and position in the water bath, ensuring they are completely underwater. Cook for 45 minutes.

- Take out the jars from the water bath and place in the refrigerator for at least 5 hours or up to 4 days.

- To serve, remove the lids and sprinkle a thin layer of sugar over the top of the crème brûlée. Caramelize the sugar using a blowtorch.

CHAPTER SIX

SOUS VIDE CHICKEN

The secret here is briefly searing the chicken in a cast-iron skillet before serving.

Ingredients

- Chicken thighs

- Salt

How to prepare

- Clip the circulator onto the side of a large stockpot and fill it with water until it reaches between the Min and Max line. Tap the screen to turn it on then rotate the green dial until the number on the bottom reads 150.0 F. The number on top is the present temperature. Allow to preheat.

- Wash and carefully dry boneless, skin-on chicken thighs. If you can only find thighs with the bone-in. Season both sides with salt and pepper. On the skinless side, place a few sprigs of your favorite herbs (here we used thyme and rosemary) along with a small pad of butter.

- Place one chicken thigh into a quart-sized (or larger) high-quality zip-top bag. We like to roll back the top so the zipper doesn't get chicken-y. Repeat for the rest of the thighs. If you're using a larger bag, you can put more than one thigh, as long as they are side-by-side and not on top of each other.

- Now we have to get all of the air out of the bags and seal them up. Fill another pot with cold water and, with the top of the bag still open, submerge the bottom of the bag into the water. This is known as the water displacement method. Keep pushing the bag into the water, allowing the water to press the air out.

- Drop all of the bags into the preheated pot and let them go for 1.5 hours. Remember, even if you forget about it for another 30 minutes (or longer), the chicken literally cannot overcook. Make sure that all the bags are submerged under water. If they aren't, just repeat the water displacement method above to ensure all the air is out.

- Just like blanching vegetables, remove the bags from the water and dunk them into a bowl filled with ice water. Chill for 10-15 minutes until cooled.

- This step is optional, but we like the results when you do it. Place the bags of chicken, skin side down, on a baking sheet. Place another baking sheet on top, weigh down with a cast iron pan or heavy cans, and allow it to sit for 30 minutes. This helps get a flatter skin that will crisp up beautifully. If you're going to eat the chicken later in the week, just transfer the bags to the fridge after this step.

- When you're ready to eat, remove the chicken from the bag and dry it very well. It may not look the most attractive now, but just wait.

- Preheat a pan (we prefer cast iron) over medium high heat, add a few tablespoons of oil, and sear the chicken skin-side down for 2-3 minutes until It is golden and crispy. Turn and cook for another 2-3 minutes. Slice, sprinkle with a touch of salt, and serve with roasted potatoes, and asparagus.

CHAPTER SEVEN

72 HOURS SOUS VIDE BBQ SHORT RIBS

Ingredients

- 3⁄4 cup unsweetened pineapple juice

- 1⁄2 cup peanut oil

- 1⁄3 cup soy sauce

- 1⁄4 cup molasses

- 1 teaspoon ground ginger

- 1 lbs short ribs

- 1 teaspoon (or more) Kosher salt and freshly ground black pepper to taste

How to prepare

BBQ Sauce

- Mix the first five ingredients, mixing well

- In a glass bowl, cover up the short ribs with the sauce. Cover and refrigerate overnight.

For sous vide

- Preheat sous vide to 54 ˚C / 131 ˚F .

- Vacuum seal the ribs, with sauce. Place into water bath and cook for 72-hours.

For slow cooker

- Add ribs with sauce to your slow cooker. Cook on LOW for 9 hours. Do not cook on high--this must be done low and slow to prevent toughness.

CHAPTER EIGHT

TAIWANESE CORN ON THE COB

Spicy, garlicky roast corn is a much loved Taiwanese street food snack--here's a quick, 20 minute version of that dish.

Ingredients

- 3 ears of summer corn
- 3 cloves garlic
- 3 Tbsp dark soy sauce
- 2 Tbsp chili sauce
- 1 Tbsp sugar
- 1 stalk green onion, rough chop
- 2 Tbsp butter
- Finishing salt

How to prepare

- Set your water bath to 85°C (185°F)
- Pour in garlic, soy sauce, chili sauce, sugar, green onions, and butter in a food processor and puree until it is smooth.

- Pour in mixture into a bag with corn and vacuum-seal. If you don't have a vacuum sealer, you can make use of a freezer-safe zip bag and seal with the water displacement method. You might need to use a weight or a wedge to keep the bag submerged underwater. Sous vide for 20 minutes.

- After 20 minutes, take out the corn from water bath. You can give the corn a nice char on the grill, broil on high for a couple minutes, or use a blow torch.

CHAPTER NINE

SOUS VIDE CHUCK-EYE STEAK DIANE

Steak Diane is rich, standard, and totally delicious — not to mention you get to play with fire.

Ingredients for 4

- 4 6-8-ounce beef chuck-eye steaks
- 1 tablespoon extra virgin olive oil
- 4 tablespoons butter
- 4 sprigs fresh thyme
- 2 tablespoons minced shallot
- 8 ounces crimini mushrooms, thinly sliced
- ¼ cup Cognac (or any decent brandy)
- 1 tablespoon Dijon mustard
- 2 teaspoons Worcestershire sauce
- 1 cup beef stock
- ½ cup heavy cream
- Kosher salt and freshly ground black pepper
- Minced fresh chives for garnish

How to prepare

- Set your Sous Vide Precision Cooker to 132°F (55.5°C).

- Season steaks generously with kosher salt.

- Seal steaks in a vacuum or Ziploc plastic bag and cook for six hours.

- Remove the steaks, reserving the cooking liquid, and pat dry.

- In a large cast-iron skillet, heat olive oil and two tablespoons of the butter over medium-high, until just beginning to smoke. Add fresh thyme and steaks and sear on both sides until dark golden brown, basting with butter and thyme as you cook. Remove steaks from the pan and set aside.

- Discard butter, oil, and thyme and add two tablespoons of fresh butter to the pan over medium heat. Add shallots and mushrooms and saute until tender, about five minutes.

- Deglaze pan with Cognac (stand back if you want to keep your eyebrows) and add mustard, Worcestershire, beef stock, and reserved cooking liquid from the bag, as well as whatever has accumulated on plate holding cooked steaks.

- Simmer sauce until reduced by half, about five minutes. Add cream and season as needed with Kosher salt and freshly ground black pepper and cook for two more minutes. (The sous vide cooking liquid will have a decent amount of salt from the steak seasoning, so taste first before adding additional salt.)

- To finish, remove pan from the heat and add steaks to the sauce, coating both sides and letting sit for about a minute to bring them back to temperature.

- Alternatively, you can slice the steaks individually and top immediately with the warm sauce. Garnish with minced chives.

CHAPTER TEN

OVERNIGHT OATMEAL WITH STEWED FRUIT COMPOTE

You can double the recipe in the same pouch for 4 servings but for more than 4 servings, make use of additional pouches

Ingredients

For the oatmeal

- 1 cup (90g) rolled oats

- 3 cups (710 ml) water

- 1 pinch salt

- 1 pinch cinnamon

For the stewed fruit compote

- ¾ cup (100g) dried fruit (any mix of the following – cherries, blueberries, golden raisins, apricots, cranberries)

- 2 tablespoons(25g) white sugar

- ½ cup (118 ml) of water

- 2 drops of vanilla extract

- 1/2 lemon, for zest, finely grated

- 1/2 orange, for zest, finely grated

How to prepare

- Fill and preheat the Sous Vide water oven to 155F/68C.

- Place a large (gallon/3.8 liter) zip-closure cooking pouch in a baggy rack. (If you don't own a baggy rack, you can always ask somebody to hold the bag open while you put in the contents.)

- Pour the oatmeal, water, salt and cinnamon into the zip-closure cooking pouch, and use the displacement method to remove the air and zip the seal closed.

- Immerse the sealed pouch in the water bath.

- Put a (quart/0.95 liter) zip-closure cooking pouch in a baggy rack and pour in the dried fruit, sugar, and water, and vanilla, orange and lemon zest. Use the displacement method to remove the air and zip the seal closed.

- Immerse the pouch in the water bath with the oatmeal.

- Six to ten hours later, take out the pouches from the water bath. Give the oatmeal pouch a fast shake and pour straight into two bowls.

- Open the pouch with the stewed fruit, spoon the fruit compote on top of the oatmeal, serve and enjoy.

CHAPTER ELEVEN

ORANGE ROSEMARY INFUSED VINEGAR

Ingredients

- 10 blood oranges (or 5 navel oranges) for zest

- 10 fresh rosemary springs

- 4 cups (.9 liters) white balsamic vinegar

How to prepare

- Fill and preheat the SousVide cooker to 153F/67C.

- Zest the oranges, being cautious to use only the orange surface of the peel, and not the white inner layer.

- In a big (gallon 3.8 liter) zip-closure cooking pouch, mix the zest with the rosemary and vinegar, evacuate the air, and zip the pouch closed.

- Submerge in the water oven and cook for 2 to 3 hours.

- Strain the vinegar through cheesecloth or a fine mesh strainer, pour into a clean bottle, and seal.

CHAPTER TWELVE

BLACKBERRY BASIL INFUSED VINEGAR

Ingredients

- 3 cups (12 oz/340 g) of blackberries

- 1/2 cup (1.3 oz/34 g) basil leaves

- 4 cups (16 fl oz/473 ml) white balsamic vinegar

How to prepare

- Fill and preheat the SousVide cooker to 153°F/ 67°C.

- Combine ingredients in a large (1 gallon/3.8 liter) zip-closure cooking pouch, evacuate the air, and zip closed.

- Immerse in the water bath and cook for 2 to 3 hours.

- Partway via the cooking process, squeeze the pouch to tenderize the blackberries.

- Strain the vinegar through cheesecloth or a fine mesh strainer and get rid of the solids.

- Pour the infusion into a clean bottle; cap tightly, label, date, and store in the refrigerator for up to six weeks.

CHAPTER THIRTEEN

CARROT AND DAIKON QUICK PICKLE

Ingredients

- 2 teaspoons (10 ml) kosher salt

- ¼ cup (48 g) sugar

- ½ cup plus 2 tablespoons (135 ml) white vinegar

- 1/2 cup (120 ml) warm water

- ½ pound carrots (228 g) peeled and cut into matchsticks

- 1 1/2 pounds daikon (228 g) peeled and cut into matchsticks

How to prepare

- Fill and preheat the SousVide cooker to 140F/60C.

- Pour the carrots and daikon into a small (quart/0.9 liter) zip-closure cooking pouch (or chamber vacuum pouch.)

- In a bowl, whisk together the salt, sugar, vinegar, and water and pour the concoction over the vegetables.

- Remove the air from the zip-closure pouch and zip the seal (or vacuum seal in the chamber vacuum.)

- Immerse the pouch in the water oven to cook for 15 minutes.

- Take out the pouch from the water oven and quick chill, immerse in an ice water bath for 15 minutes.

- Refrigerate for use within 4 weeks.

CHAPTER FOURTEEN

CHOCOLATE ZABAGLIONE

Ingredients

- 8 large egg yolks

- 1 cup (192 g) sugar

- Pinch salt

- 1/2 cup (120 ml) dry Marsala

- 1/3 cup (37 g) unsweetened cocoa powder

- 1/4 cup (60 ml) whipping cream, or heavy cream

- 1 pound (0.45 kg) fresh strawberries, washed, hulled, and quartered

How to prepare

- Fill and preheat the SousVide cooker to 165F/74C.

- In the meantime, in a bowl, whisk together the egg yolks, sugar, salt and Marsala.

- Add in cocoa powder and whisk until it is totally combined, then add cream and whisk well.

- Pour the egg mixture into a large (gallon/3.8 liter) zip-closure cooking pouch.

- Remove the air from the pouch and zip the seal.

- Immerse the pouch in the water oven to cook for 20 to 30 minutes until it is thick and creamy. Occasionally, lift the pouch from the water bath and massage the contents through the pouch to mix and return to the water.

- Meanwhile, divide the strawberries among individual dessert bowls or stemmed cocktail glasses.

- When ready to serve, pour the warm zabaglione over the strawberries, or if you desire, pour the zabaglione into individual serving bowls, cover, and chill until set in the refrigerator, then garnish each bowl with a few fresh strawberries at serving.

CHAPTER FIFTEEN

VANILLA BEAN ICE CREAM

Ingredients

- 6 large egg yolks

- 1 cup (75 g) superfine (castor) sugar

- 1/4 cup (29 g) non-fat dry milk powder (organic if available)

- 1 quart (.9 liter) half-and-half

- 1/2 vanilla bean

How to prepare

- Fill and preheat the water oven to 140F/60C.

- In a bowl, beat the egg yolks with the sugar and non-fat dry milk until it is light yellow and thickened.

- Scrape the seeds from the vanilla bean and add them and the half and half to the yolks and beat just enough to mix.

- Pour the concoction into a large (gallon/3.8 liter) zip-closure cooking pouch; remove the air from the pouch and zip it closed. (If you are using standard vacuum seal pouches, press out as much air as possible from the pouch with your hands and seal only. Do not attempt to seal liquids using a suction vacuum sealer.)

- Immerse the pouch in the water oven and cook for 45 minutes to 1 hour.

- Remove the pouch from the water bath and quick chill it, immersed in ice water (half ice/half water) for 30 minutes. Refrigerate until ready to churn.

- Churn the chilled mixture according to your ice cream machine's manufacturer's instructions.

- Serve immediately, or if you want, scoop into a quart container, cover it tightly, and freeze for one hour before serving if you desire a firmer consistency.

CHAPTER SIXTEEN

SOUS VIDE CORNED BEEF AND CABBAGE

Ingredients

- 4 pounds (1.81 kg) of corned beef

- 6 slices of bacon, cut into ½ inch (1.3 cm) strips

- 1 head of cabbage, cut into 1-inch (3 cm) strips

- 2 cups (470 ml) chicken stock

- 1/2 cup (120 ml) champagne vinegar

How to prepare

- Pre-heat the water oven to 134°F/56°C.

- Put the corned beef into a cooking pouch and vacuum/seal.

- Immerse the pouch in the water oven and cook for 48 hours

- About 45 minutes before you are ready to serve the meal, prepare the cabbage.

- In a skillet, over medium heat, cook the bacon pieces until they are crisp and the fat is rendered. Pour off all but 1-2 tablespoons (15 to 30 ml) of the bacon fat.

- Add in the cabbage strips to the skillet, raise the heat to medium-high, and cook for about 5 minutes.

- Add the chicken stock and the vinegar to the pan and continue to cook the cabbage in the liquid until tender.

- When the cabbage is almost tender, remove the corned beef from the water bath and the cooking pouch.

- To serve, slice the corned beef into 1/2" – 3/4" (1.3 cm – 2 cm) slices and serve over the cabbage.

CHAPTER SEVENTEEN

SOUS VIDE BROWN BUTTER SCALLOPS

Ingredients

- 1 package SizzleFish Scallops (about 4.25oz)

- 2 tsp brown butter (1 tsp for cooking + 1 tsp for searing)*

- salt & pepper, as desired

How to prepare

- Fill up your pot with water

- Preheat the sous vide circulator to 140 degrees

- Pat your scallops dry with a paper towel

- Place scallops, 1 tsp brown butter, salt and pepper in a ziploc bag

- Seal tight, making sure to remove all air

- Put the bag in the water and ensure that it stays underwater

- Set timer for 35 minutes (They can take up to 40 minutes)

- Once done, take out from the water and bag

- Pat the scallops dry

- Heat up your left over tsp of brown butter in a pan over high heat

- Add your scallops to the pan to get a golden sear (about 30 seconds per side)

- Serve as desired

Notes

- Feel free to use any oil you choose

CHAPTER EIGHTEEN

SOUS-VIDE CHAR SIU

Ingredients

- 1kg Berkshire or Kurobuta pork neck

- Marinade

- 6 scallions, sliced into 2 inch lengths and smashed

- 8 garlic cloves, smashed and peeled

- 3 tablespoons regular soy sauce

- 2 tablespoons Chinese rice wine

- 3 tablespoons sugar

- 2.5 tablespoons hoisin sauce

- 2 tablespoons rich chicken stock

- 1 teaspoon sesame oil

How to prepare

- Mix all the marinade ingredients together well.

- Cut the pork lengthwise into strips around 2.5-3 inches wide and 2 inches or so thick. Cut strips diagonally, if needed, into pieces 6-8 inches long. Position it in a big baking dish that can accommodate all the pork in one layer. Pour the marinade atop the pork. Seal the dish with cling wrap overnight, at least 12 hours and up to 36 hours. Turn the pork a few times during the marinating process. Keep in the fridge.

- Prepare a water bath, using an immersion circulator, and bring the water to 58 degrees Celsius

- Place each piece of pork, with some marinade, into a vacuum-sealable bag and seal at high pressure.

- Drop the bags into the water bath and cook for 24 hours. Once done, prepare an ice water bath and plunge the bags of pork directly into the ice water. Once cool, dry off the bags and either freeze or put in the fridge. Or open the bags, liberate your pork, and move to the final step of finishing off the pork.

Finishing Sauce (enough for two strips)

- 1 teaspoon salt

- 1 tablespoon hoisin sauce

- 2 teaspoons honey

How to prepare

- Mix the above together and taste. It should be salty-sweet.

- Preheat your oven to the highest temperature it can go. Pour some water into a roasting pan. Over the pan, place a large wire rack that fits over the top of the pan.

- Brush as much of the finishing sauce onto the strips of pork. You want it thick. Lay the pork on the wire rack (and over the water in the roasting pan). Pop this in the oven for 10 minutes or until the surface of the char siu is nicely charred.

- Alternatively, instead of using the oven, blowtorch the pork until charred.

CHAPTER NINETEEN

SOUS VIDE SESAME SALMON WITH SOBA NOODLES

Ingredients

For salmon:

- 2 (6-ounce) sashimi-grade salmon filets, with skin

- Salt and pepper

- 1 teaspoon sesame oil

- 1 cup extra virgin olive oil

- 1 tablespoon fresh ginger, grated

- 2 tablespoons honey

For sesame soba:

- 4 ounces dry soba noodles

- 1 tablespoon grape seed oil

- 2 cloves of garlic, chopped

- 1/2 head of broccoli

- 3 tablespoons tahini

- 1 teaspoon sesame oil

- 2 teaspoons extra virgin olive oil

- 1/4 lime, juiced

- 1 stalk green onion, sliced

- 1/4 cup cilantro, roughly chopped

- 1 teaspoon toasted sesame seeds

- Sesame seeds and lime wedges, for garnish

How to prepare

- Set up sous vide water bath, and set temperature of the sous vide to 51°C (123.8°F).

- In a medium-sized mixing bowl, mix up sesame oil, olive oil, ginger, and honey. In a quart-sized freezer-safe zip bag, add seasoned filets and seasoning mixture. Seal and sous vide at 51°C (123.8°F) for 20 minutes.

- While the fish is cooking, prepare soba noodles according to package directions.

- In the meantime, in a skillet over medium-high heat, heat grape seed oil. Stir-fry garlic and broccoli until soft, about 6-8 minutes.

- In a small mixing bowl, whisk together tahini, sesame oil, olive oil, lime juice, green onions, cilantro, and toasted sesame seeds. Mix into cooked and drained soba noodles, and toss in stir-fried broccoli and garlic.

- Heat a skillet over medium-high heat. Position a piece of parchment paper on the bottom of the skillet (the parchment paper will keep the skin from sticking to the pan). Turn up the heat to high, and transfer salmon to the pan, skin side down. Sear until skin is crisp, about 30 seconds to 1 minute.

- Divide soba noodles into two bowls; top with salmon, sesame seeds, and a lime wedge.

CHAPTER TWENTY

PORK TENDERLOIN WITH ROSEMARY GARLIC MAPLE GLAZE

The rosemary garlic maple rub is so delicious. It is highly recommended to make extra to glaze after cooking and add to your apple / onion hash.

Ingredients

- 1 1lb pork tenderloin

- ½ pink lady (or other tart) apple, cut into small cubes

- ½ large white or yellow onion, diced

- 1 tsp butter

- Rosemary Garlic Maple glaze

- 3 large sprigs rosemary

- 2 garlic cloves, mashed into a paste

- ¼ cup olive oil

- 1 tbsp maple syrup

- Large pinch salt

How to prepare

- Preheat sous vide machine to 135 degrees F.

- Mix all glaze ingredients in a food processor.

- Set aside nearly 1/3 of the mixture. Use the rest to rub all over pork loin. Add in some additional salt to the loin. Vacuum seal loin and place into the 135 F water bath. Cook for 2.5 hours.

- Take out pork from bag. Heat a nonstick skillet with butter until sizzling. Add in pork and sear, rotating, so all sides get a toasty brown, about 45-60 seconds / side. Take out pork and set aside.

- Using the same skillet, add your apples and onions and a tbsp of the reserved glaze.

- Slice pork, spooning any extra glaze on top. Serve with a rich scoop of apple and onion hash. Salt more to taste if necessary

CHAPTER TWENTY ONE

SOUS VIDE CHEESECAKE

Ingredients

- 16 oz Cream Cheese

- 3 Eggs

- ¾ Cup Sugar

- ½ tbs. Vanilla Extract

- ¼ Cup Sour Cream

- Fruit to top, if desired

Crust

- ½ Package of Graham Crackers (About 4-5), Crushed

- 1 tbs. Sugar

- 3 tbs. Unsalted Butter, Melted

- ¼ Tsp Cinnamon

How to prepare

- Preheat water bath to 176F.

- Crush graham crackers into very fine pieces. I place them in a sandwich bag and use a rolling pin.

- Add sugar, melted butter, and cinnamon. Mix thoroughly.

- Place crust mixture at the bottom of 8 4oz canning jars and firmly pack down.

- (Optional) Bake crust and jars for 10 minutes at 350F.

- Add room temperature cream cheese, eggs, sugar, sour cream, and vanilla into a large mixing bowl and mix thoroughly.

- Add cheesecake mixture to each canning jar, leaving about ½ inch from the top.

- Tighten canning jar lids using ONLY your fingertips, ensuring not to fully tighten as air must escape during the cooking process.

- Cook for 1 hour 30 minutes.

- Carefully remove from water bath using tongs and let chill on the counter until cool to touch (about 1 hour).

- Place cheesecakes in refrigerator for at least 4 hours.

- Open lid, top with fresh fruit or blueberry filling, and enjoy!

CHAPTER TWENTY TWO

SOUS VIDE BONELESS PORK CHOP

Pork is the unsung hero in the sous vide world. When it comes to sous vide boneless pork chops, the thicker the better.

Ingredients

- Thick cut boneless pork chops

- Salt and pepper

- (optional) Marinade of Choice

How to prepare

- (Optional) Marinate pork chops for 24 hours.

- Pre-heat water bath to your ideal temperature. We prefer 140°F.

- Vacuum seal the pork or put it in a heavy duty Ziploc bag using the water displacement method.

- Put packaged pork chop in water bath and cook for 1.5 - 3 hours.

- Take out pork chop and pat dry with paper towels.

- Pre-heat cast iron pan on medium-high heat and add avocado oil (or high smoke point oil).

- Sear on hot cast iron pan using for 1 minute, flipping every 15 seconds.

- Add butter and any aromatics to the pan for additional flavor and crispness. Sear for an additional 30 or so.

- (Optional) Break out the searing torch if you're feeling adventurous for a perfect crust.

- If you want, serve with pan sauce made from bag juices and remaining marinade.

CHAPTER TWENTY THREE

SOUS VIDE SHORT RIBS

Beef short ribs have the largest array of possible textures and flavor profiles out of any meat cooked sous vide. A 72 hour cook at 130F delivers a texture you've never experienced before, while 24 hours at 165F delivers a traditional yet juicy texture. This is absolutely one of the most transformational uses of sous vide.

Ingredients

- Beef Short Ribs (2-4)

- Sea Salt

- Cracked Black Pepper

- Garlic Powder

- Avocado Oil (or another high smoke point oil)

How to prepare

- Usually an elective step of marinating beforehand, but because this recipe cooks for a minimum of 24 hours, the beef will marinate in its juices and whatever spices you add - perfect!

- Pre-heat water bath to your ideal temperature. We recommend 165°F for a traditional, yet juicy, texture;

however, the famous 72 hour short rib is also a masterpiece.

- Generously season with sea salt, cracked black pepper, a pinch of garlic powder, and any aromatics such as rosemary or thyme.

- Vacuum seal the short ribs. Or if you're cooking the 48 hour or 72 hour recipe, you can place it in a heavy duty Ziploc bag using the water displacement method since the temperatures are low enough. Temperatures over 155F can break the seal of Ziploc bags.

- Remove ribs and pat dry with paper towels, saving the juice from the bag.

- Using a cheese cloth, filter the juice into a saucepan and lessen by half at a simmer.

- Pre-heat cast iron pan on medium-high heat and add avocado oil (or another high smoke point oil).

- Sear ribs on hot cast iron pan for about 1 minute, flipping every 15 seconds.

- Add butter and any aromatics to the pan for added flavor and crispness. Sear for an

- (Optional) Break out the searing torch if you're feeling adventurous for a perfect crust.

- Plate beef short ribs with juice reduction.

CHAPTER TWENTY FOUR

SOUS VIDE SAUSAGE

Sous vide sausage is unbelievably juicy and is one of the only meats that taste awesome right from the bag without having to worry about searing.

Ingredients

- Sausage

- (Optional) Beer, Beef Stock

How to prepare

- Pre-heat water bath to 160F depending on your preference. 140F will be very juicy and soft, 150F will be juicy and firm, 160F will be like the conventional but still more juicy.

- Vacuum seal your sausage or use Ziploc freezer bags with the water displacement method. (Optional) if you plan on eating the sausage plain and/or on a bun, you can add a light beer and some beef broth to your bag during the cook.

- Cook for 1-2 hours.

- Take out sausage from bag, discard juices, and pat dry with paper towels.

- If eating as an appetizer or on a bun, you can quickly sear it on a grill or cast iron. However, sous vide sausage is one of few meats that taste great right from the bag!

CHAPTER TWENTY FIVE

SOUS VIDE HALIBUT

Halibut is traditionally a firm fish, which makes it great for searing. Since the fish is normally pretty firm, it also tends to become really dry with conventional cooking methods. Sous vide lets you ensure the halibut stays absolutely moist and flaky, while still being able to obtain an amazing golden brown sear.

Ingredients

- 2 Halibut Filets; I ordered mine from Omaha Steaks.

- 2 tbs.Butter

- Fresh Dill

- Lemon

- Salt

- Pepper

- Olive Oil

Temperature

[140F for 45 minutes] Traditional texture (a bit tougher) much more dry than the temperatures below.

[130F for 45 minutes] It is moist but still firm enough to sear it without worrying about it falling apart.

[120F for 45 minutes] Most tender, but still nearly raw.

How to prepare

- Dry brine halibut by richly salting both sides (and use a 50/50 ratio of salt/sugar) and place back in refrigerator for at least 30 minutes or up to 24 hours.

- Preheat water bath to your desired temperature shown above; I prefer 130F.

- Carefully place the halibut filets in a Ziploc bag. Add in a bit of oil and fresh dill to the bag. Place into the water bath using the water displacement technique.

- Cook for 45 minutes, or about an hour and 15 minutes if frozen.

- Take out from water bath and tenderly pat the halibut dry with paper towels. This is crucial for obtaining a nice quick sear.

- Pre-heat a cast iron or stainless steel pan with avocado oil on medium-high/high heat.

- Add halibut, followed by a tablespoon or two of butter and fresh herbs.

- Baste the halibut with butter as it cooks, 1-2 minutes (you only need to sear the one side).

- Remove and serve!

CHAPTER TWENTY SIX

SOUS VIDE POACHED EGGS + AVOCADO TOAST

This worthy breakfast is just as healthy as it is tasty, and sous vide makes poached eggs a breeze. In just 15 minutes, you can have constantly perfect, gooey eggs, every single time.

Ingredients

- 2 - 4 Eggs

- Avocado Toast

- 2 slices of bread, toasted (I prefer rye)

- 1 Avocado, sliced or spread on bread (if you opt to slice instead of spread, I recommend spreading some butter on the toast)

- Salt (I like to use a chili lime sea salt)

- Pepper

- Chives

How to prepare

- Preheat water bath to 167F

- Gently lower your eggs into the water, ensuring not to crack. I use a pair of kitchen tongs.

- Cook for 15 minutes.

- Remove eggs and run them under cold tap water for 30 seconds or so to prevent them from overcooking.

- Place avocado on toast and top with salt, pepper, and chives.

- Gently crack an egg or two over your toast and enjoy!

CHAPTER TWENTY SEVEN

SOUS VIDE COD

Cod (and salmon) do not require a finishing sear once it's done cooking, so it can't get any easier! Just bag the cod filets with some butter, dill, lemon, and capers, and cook for 45 minutes. You can even melt your serving butter right in the water bath along with the fish!

Ingredients

- 2 Cod Filets

- 2 tbs. Butter

- Fresh Dill

- (Optional) Lemon and Capers

- Salt

- Pepper

How to prepare

- Preheat water bath to your desired temperature shown above; I prefer 130F.

- Gently place the cod filets in a Ziploc bag. Add in 2tbps of butter and some fresh dill to the bag. Optionally, you can also add a few slices of lemon and capers into the bag.

- Put bag into the water bath using the water displacement method.

- Cook for 45 minutes, or about an hour and 15 minutes if frozen.

- Take it out and serve! Cod, much like salmon, does not require a sear like most meats we cook sous vide.

CHAPTER TWENTY EIGHT

SOUS VIDE COLD BREW COFFEE

Thanks to sous vide, cold brew coffee no longer needs to take 24 hours to make! We can cut the brewing time down to 2 hours and have the same tasting results. Give this sous vide cold brew coffee recipe a try!

Ingredients

- 3/4 Cup Fresh, Coarsely Ground Coffee

- 4 Cups of Water

- 2 16oz Mason Jars (or smaller sizes equaling to 32oz)

How to prepare

- Grind your fresh coffee beans on a very coarse setting - finely ground coffee can end up cloudy when cold brewing.

- Pour the coffee grounds and water to a large bowl and stir until all coffee grounds are soaked.

- Equally pour the coffee mixture into your mason jars ensuring to leave at least a half inch of room from the top.

- Put the lids on the mason jars and ONLY tighten with your finger tips. Over-tightening the lid can break the glass, as air needs to escape when heating.

- Immerse the mason jars into a pre-heated water bath at 150F for about 2 hours.

- Take out jars, filter the coffee with either a coffee filter or cheese cloth, and chill in the fridge.

- (Optional) The coffee will be quite strong as is - if it's too strong for your tastes, dilute the coffee by adding more cold water, up to a 1:1 ratio.

- Pour and serve over ice!

CHAPTER TWENTY NINE

SOUS VIDE GARLIC HERB BUTTER STEAK

These steaks are so delicious, juicy and evenly cooked. Sous vide is a really exciting method to explore as a home cook.

Ingredients

- 4 Filet Mignon Steaks about 1/2 pound each

- Kosher salt

- Freshly ground pepper

- Garlic powder

- 2 tablespoons of butter

- 1 clove of garlic finely minced

- 2 tablespoons of chopped fresh flat leaf parsley

- 1-2 tablespoon of vegetable oil

How to prepare

- Season steaks to taste with salt, pepper and a small amount of garlic powder.

- Heat Sous Vide to temperature based on preference of doneness, from rare, medium-rare or medium. Refer to chart in directions for temp and time guidelines.

- If preference is medium-rare, heat water bath to 130 degrees to account for increase in temp during final searing and set timer for one hour.

- When water is heated, submerge steaks in plastic storage bag and seal.

- While steaks are cooking, prepare garlic butter.

- Mix softened butter with minced garlic, pinch of salt and parsley.

- Remove steaks from water bath after one hour.

- Heat cast iron skillet over high heat with 1-2 tablespoon of olive oil. Once oil is smoking, quickly sear steaks on each side. 30 second to 1 minute per side.

- Top the steaks with butter compound, let it rest and serve.

CHAPTER THIRTY

SOUS VIDE CARROTS

Cooking carrots sous vide prevents all the flavor and nutrients leaching out, resulting in crunchy, flavorsome carrots every time.

Ingredients

- Carrot
- Olive oil
- Salt

How to prepare

- Preheat the water bath to 85°C
- Place a single layer of baby carrots in a vacuum bag and add a little olive oil and a pinch of salt
- Vacuum seal the bag and place it in the preheated water bath to cook for 25 minutes
- Take out the carrots from the bag and drain on kitchen paper. Serve immediately with a knob of butter

CHAPTER THIRTY ONE

SOUS VIDE LAMB CHOPS WITH BASIL CHIMICHURRI

Ingredients:

Lamb chops

- 2 rack of lamb, frenched

- 2 cloves garlic, crushed

- Salt

- pepper

Basil Chimichurri

- 1 cup fresh basil, finely chopped

- 1 shallot diced

- 1-2 clove of garlic, minced

- 1 ts red chili flakes

- 1/2 olive oil

- 3 tbs. red wine vinegar

- 1/4 tbs.sea salt

- 1/4 tbs. pepper

How to prepare

- Set sous vide temperature to 56 degrees Celsius. Season lamb liberally with salt and pepper. Vacuum seal lamb with crush garlic and sous vide for 2 hours.

- Combine all of the ingredients of the basil chimichurri sauce in bowl and mix well. Season to taste and cover and refrigerate to let flavors blend together.

- After two hours, remove lamb chops from bag and dry well with paper towel. Sear with torch or scalding hot well oiled pan. Slice the between the bones and liberally top with basil chimichurri sauce and enjoy.

CHAPTER THIRTY TWO

SOUS VIDE DUCK LEGS

Ingredients

- 4 duck legs

- Kosher salt and freshly ground black pepper

- 4 medium cloves garlic, minced

- 4 sprigs thyme

How to prepare

- Set up an immersion circulator and preheat the water bath to 155°F (68°C).

- Season duck all over with salt and pepper. Rub garlic onto the meaty side of each leg and set a thyme sprig on top. Slide duck legs into vacuum bags and seal according to vacuum-sealer manufacturer's instructions.

- Add sealed duck to water bath and cook for 36 hours. Make sure to top water up periodically as it evaporates, and keep bag totally underwater. If bag floats, weigh it down by placing a wet kitchen towel on top of it.

- Take out duck from water bath and transfer to a refrigerator to chill. The duck can be kept refrigerated within the sealed bag for up to 1 week.

- When ready to use, take out duck from bag and scrape away thyme sprigs and excess fat and juices. Use duck confit according to any recipe you have; it can be cooked in a 450°F (230°C) oven or broiled until the meat is heated through and the skin is browned and crispy, about 7 minutes.

CHAPTER THIRTY THREE

SOUS VIDE SPICED AUBERGINE WITH TURMERIC AND COCONUT SAUCE, CASHEW BUTTER AND CRISPY KALE

Ingredients

Sous vide aubergine

- 6 baby aubergines

- 1/2 tsp coriander seeds

- 1/2 tsp fennel seeds

- 1/2 tsp cumin seeds

- 50ml of olive oil

- table salt

- sea salt

- freshly ground black pepper

Kale crisps

- 200g of kale

- 1 tbsp of olive oil

- 1 tbsp of cashew nuts

- table salt

Turmeric and coconut sauce

- 20g of fresh turmeric, sliced

- 2 shallots, sliced

- 1 knob of ginger, 3cm in length, peeled and sliced

- 20g of cashew nuts, toasted

- 1/4 bunch of coriander stalks

- 400ml of coconut milk

- 1 dash of vegetable oil

Cashew butter

- 100g of cashew nuts, toasted

- 100ml of warm water

- Salt

How to prepare

For the kale crisps, rub the oil into the leaves and season well with table salt. Microplane the cashew nuts over the kale and place in a dehydrator or 60°C oven overnight to crisp up

- For the aubergine, preheat the water bath to 72°C

- Put the coriander, fennel and cumin seeds in a dry frying pan over a medium heat and toast until it is fragrant, lightly crush and mix with the olive oil

- Halve the aubergines lengthwise and score the flesh in a crisscross pattern. Season it generously with table salt and leave for 10 minutes. After 10 minutes, wipe away the salt and any excess moisture

- Put the aubergines in 2 vacuum bags and add the spiced oil. Seal, being careful not to take all of the air out as you will crush the aubergines, and place in the water bath for 90 minutes

- For the turmeric and coconut sauce, heat a dash of vegetable oil in a large saucepan. When hot, add all the ingredients apart from the coconut milk. Season well, cook for 10 minutes until lightly colored then add the coconut milk

- Simmer for 20 minutes then place in a blender and blitz until smooth. Pass through a fine sieve

- For the cashew butter, place the cashew nuts in a blender, season well and add the warm water. Blend until smooth, adding a little more water if necessary. Transfer to a piping bag

- Remove the aubergines from the bags and season with a little sea salt and pepper

- Plate the aubergines with dots of cashew butter, drizzles of turmeric sauce and pieces of crispy kale

CHAPTER THIRTY FOUR

SOUS VIDE BRUSSELS SPROUTS AND SPROUT TOPS, MISO BUTTER, CASHEW

Ingredients

- 16 Brussels sprouts

- 1kg sprout tops, hard stalks removed

- 2 bay leaves

- 30g miso paste

- 100g unsalted butter

- 80g roasted cashew nuts, chopped

- 1 tbsp chopped tarragon leaves

How to prepare

- Preheat your water to 70^0C 1

- Start by making the miso butter. Tip the miso paste into a bowl along with the butter and whisk together.

- Prep the sprouts by chopping off the bottom and if large, cut in half so that they are all approximately the same size. Move the sprouts to a vacuum bag along with a couple of bay leaves and half of the miso butter.

- Vacuum seal the pouch and pop into the water bath to sous vide for 45 minutes. 4

- Place the sprout tops into a separate vacuum bag along with the remaining half of the miso butter. Seal and put into the water bath for the last 20 minutes of cooking.

- To arrange the dish, take the cooked sprouts from the bath and mix in a bowl with the cashew nuts and tarragon leaves.

CHAPTER THIRTY FIVE

SOUS VIDE LEEKS

Cooking leeks can be difficult because the outer layers cook faster than the inner core. This makes it hard to achieve a uniform result. You can avoid this problem by cooking leeks sous vide in a water bath. In this technique, the low cooking temperature means that the leeks never go beyond the optimum temperature, which prevents them from overcooking on the outside.

Ingredients

- 3 large leeks, trimmed with base intact

- 25ml of olive oil

- salt

How to prepare

- Preheat the water bath to a temperature of 85^0C. 1

- Arrange the leeks side by side in a vacuum bag. Season it with salt, pour over the olive oil and vacuum the bag to seal

- Put the bag in the water bath and leave it to cook for around 30 minutes. To test if the leeks are cooked, give them a gentle squeeze; if they feel tender, they are ready.

- Slide the leeks out of the vacuum bag and drain it on kitchen paper

CHAPTER THIRTY SIX

POLENTA SOUS VIDE

If you are looking for a delicious substitute to wheat or potato, polenta – at times known as cornmeal – is a great choice. However, cooking polenta in the conventional way using a saucepan can be difficult: the polenta can stick to the base of the pan and, unless it is stirred very frequently, it can form a horrible skin. You can evade these common problems by cooking polenta sous vide.

How to prepare

- Preheat the water bath to a temperature of 85^0C.

- Position the polenta in a large bowl and add the water, butter and parmesan. Stir until thoroughly combined.

- Seal the mixture inside a vacuum bag.

- Put the bag in the water bath and leave it to cook for 2 hours.

- Tip the cooked polenta out of the vacuum bag into a bowl. It is now ready to be served.

CHAPTER THIRTY SEVEN

SOUS VIDE FENNEL AND ORANGE QUINOA SALAD

Ingredients

Quinoa and fennel salad

- 100g of quinoa

- 500ml of vegetable stock

- 1 fennel bulb, cut into eighths

- 50ml of orange juice

- 1 pinch of saffron

- 2 tbsp of pomegranate seeds

- 1 tsp sesame seeds, toasted

- 2 tsp fresh coriander, finely chopped

- 3 tbsp of extra virgin olive oil

- 1 tbsp of lemon vinegar

- salt

- freshly ground black pepper

Toasted pine nuts

- 2 tsp pine nuts

- 1 pinch of salt

Tahini Dressing

- 1 tbsp of tahini

- 20ml of lemon juice

- 50ml of olive oil

- 6 orange segments

- nasturtium leaves

- coriander cress

How to prepare

- First, cook the quinoa. Put the quinoa in a medium sized saucepan and pour over the vegetable stock. Heat until the stock reaches the boil, then simmer until the quinoa is cooked al dente. This should take around 15 minutes. Once cooked, take the pan off the heat and set aside to cool.

- Preheat the water bath to a temperature of 85^{0}C.

- To prepare the fennel, seal the fennel wedges inside a vacuum bag with the orange juice and the saffron. Place the bag in the water bath and leave to cook for 20 minutes.

- Unseal and drain the vacuum bag. Lay the cooked fennel in a hot frying pan. Cook over a high heat until browned on one side, then turn over and brown the other side. Add the seared fennel to the quinoa and mix in the pomegranate seeds, toasted sesame seeds and chopped coriander.

- Prepare a lemon dressing for the salad by thoroughly combining the olive oil and lemon vinegar in a small bowl. Drizzle a small amount of dressing over the quinoa, followed by a sprinkling of salt and pepper, and mix well. Taste the salad to check the flavor and seasoning. If desired, add a little more dressing.

- To make the toasted pine nuts, warm a frying pan over a low heat. Scatter the pine nuts over the base of the pan and fry gently until lightly toasted all over. To season, add a pinch of salt to the pan and shake vigorously.

- Just before serving, make the tahini dressing. Place the tahini, lemon juice and olive oil in a small bowl and mix together using a whisk.

- To serve, spoon an equal amount of quinoa and fennel salad onto each plate. Scatter the toasted pine nuts, orange segments, nasturtium leaves and coriander cress over the salad, then finish the dish with a drizzle of tahini dressing.

CHAPTER THIRTY EIGHT

BEETROOT WITH PICKLED QUINCE

Ingredients

Quince pickles

- 1 quince, peeled

- 250g of white balsamic vinegar

- 250g of Chardonnay vinegar

- 230g of water

- 1 sprig of lemon verbena

- Cheltenham beetroot

- 4 Cheltenham beetroot

- 25g of olive oil

- 1 sprig of thyme

- salt

- pepper

Marinated beetroot

- 1 baby golden beetroot

- 1 baby white beetroot

- 16 spinach leaves

- 1 handful of chervil

- olive oil

- salt

How to prepare

- To prepare the pickled quince, mix the white balsamic vinegar, Chardonnay vinegar, water and lemon verbena in a saucepan and heat it until the mixture reaches the boil, then allow to cool slightly. Place the quince in a vacuum bag and pour over the warm pickling liquid. Vacuum the bag in a chamber sealer and set aside for 24 hours to pickle.

- Preheat the oven to a temperature of 180^0C/gas mark 4.

- Rub the Cheltenham beetroot with olive oil and season it with salt and pepper, then arrange it on a baking tray and scatter over the thyme.

- Put the baking tray in the oven and cook until the beetroot are heated through but still firm. This should take about 30 minutes. Once cooked, take the tray out of the oven. Set aside to cool a little, then peel the beetroot, reserving the skins, and slice the flesh into thirds.

- In a blender, purée the skins from the Cheltenham beetroot. Put the purée in a covered container and keep warm until ready to serve.

- To make the marinated beetroot, cut the baby beetroot into thin slices. Unseal the vacuum bag containing the quince and remove the fruit, then pour the pickling liquid over the sliced beetroot and leave to marinate.

- Finely dice the pickled quince.

- When you are ready to serve, heat a dash of olive oil in a saucepan, add the spinach leaves and gently sauté until just wilted. Sprinkle a pinch of salt over the wilted leaves to season.

- To serve, smear a spoonful or two of beetroot purée over the base of each plate and top with one of the Cheltenham beetroot. Scatter the diced quince and marinated baby beetroot around the plate, add 4 spinach leaves and finish with a garnish of chervil sprigs.

CHAPTER THIRTY NINE

SOUS VIDE POTATO RÖSTI

Ingredients

- 2kg Maris Piper potatoes, grated

- 120g of duck fat, plus extra for pan-frying

- salt, to season generously

How to prepare

- Preheat the water bath to a temperature of 80^{0}C.

- Throw the grated potato with the salt, then put in a colander and set aside to drain. The salt will draw out the starchy water in potato.

- After 15 minutes, wrap the potato in a clean, dry tea towel. Twist the tea towel until you cannot squeeze out any more moisture, then move the potato to a mixing bowl.

- Heat the duck fat in a small saucepan until it is completely melted. Tip the molten fat into the bowl with the grated potato and stir until thoroughly mixed, then seal the mixture in a large vacuum bag using a chamber sealer.

- Put the bag in the water bath and cook for 4 hours.

- Once it is cooked, leave the potato to cool inside the vacuum bag. When it has cooled completely, unseal the bag, remove the rösti and divide into 8 portions. You can make the portions any shape you choose.

- Melt some duck fat in a frying pan; add the portions of rösti and fry, turning as necessary, until golden brown and crispy all over.

CHAPTER FORTY

PUMPKIN VELOUTÉ WITH WILD MUSHROOMS

Ingredients

- 1kg pumpkin

- 100g of butter

- 10ml of truffle oil

- salt

Wild mushrooms

- 250g of girolles mushrooms

- vegetable oil

- 1 knob of butter

- sea salt

- 10g of chives, chopped

- pumpkin seeds, roasted – to serve

- truffle, grated – to serve

How to prepare

- Preheat the water bath to a temperature of 90°C.

- To make the pumpkin, remove its outer skin, then cut the flesh into wedges and scoop out the seeds.

- Slice the wedges on a mandoline to make thin slivers of pumpkin. Season it with salt, and then seal half the pumpkin slivers, butter and truffle oil in one vacuum bag and half in another. Place both vacuum bags in the water bath and leave to cook for 90 minutes.

- Move the cooked pumpkin into a blender and pulse to make a smooth and glossy velouté. If the velouté is very thick, loosen it with a splash of water. Add salt to taste and store it in a warm place until needed. Do not allow the velouté to cool.

- Rinse the mushrooms in plenty of cold water, then leave to drain on kitchen paper. When the mushrooms are clean and dry, carefully strip the skin off the stems with a small knife.

- In very hot frying pan, fry the mushrooms with a dash of oil until it is lightly browned, and then stir in the butter, flaky sea salt and chopped chives.

- To serve, put a few mushrooms in the centre of each bowl, keeping about a third in reserve. Spoon the velouté into the bowls, then finish the dish by scattering the roasted pumpkin seeds, grated truffle and remaining mushrooms over the top.

CHAPTER FORTY ONE

PICKLED RADISH, DILL EMULSION AND PUFFED QUINOA

Ingredients

Dill emulsion

- 3 bunches of dill

- 300ml of sunflower oil

- 50ml of cider vinegar

- 3 egg yolks

- salt to season

Dill powder

- 1 bunch of dill

Quinoa

- 100g of quinoa

- 500ml of vegetable oil

Pickled radishes

- 1 bunch of radishes

- 200ml of white wine vinegar

- 100ml of water

- 50g of sugar

How to prepare

- To make the dill emulsion, begin by blanching the dill in boiling water then shocking it in cold water to stop the cooking process.

- Dry the dill as thoroughly as possible. Mix with the oil and liquidize in a blender.

- Suspend a muslin bag over a large jug. Pour the dill oil into the bag and leave it to strain into the jug overnight.

- Next, make the dill powder. To do this, place the dill in a dehydrator. Leave it to dry for 3 hours then take it out from the dehydrator and reduce it to a fine powder with the use of a blender.

- Bring a large pan of water to the boil and add in the quinoa. Simmer it until it is soft, then refresh the quinoa in cold water and place it in a dehydrator. Dry until it is crispy.

- To pickle the radishes, place them in a vacuum bag. Combine the white wine vinegar, water and sugar and pour over the radishes, then seal the bag using a chamber sealer. Leave to pickle for 1 hour, then open the bag, drain off the pickling liquid and set the radishes to one side.

- To finish up the dill emulsion, combine together the cider vinegar and egg yolk with the use of a whisk. When they are thoroughly combined, very gradually add the dill oil. Keep whisking until all the oil has been added and the mixture is smooth and emulsified. Add salt to taste.

- Preheat a deep-fryer to a temperature of 210^{0}C. When this temperature has been reached, add the dehydrated quinoa and fry until golden.

- To serve it, divide the pickled radishes between two plates. Pour some of the dill emulsion onto each plate, scatter the quinoa over the top and finish with a dusting of dill powder.

CHAPTER FORTY TWO

SOUS VIDE PIGS EARS

Pig's ears are a sadly underrated and the most underused part of the pig. Cooked properly, they are a very delicious savory treat and, when fried and crispy, they make a great canape. Furthermore, because the demand is low, they are usually very cheap, although you may have to order them in advance from your butcher.

Ingredients

- 4 pig's ears

- 50g of rock salt

- 50ml of vegetable oil

- Rice flour, for dusting

How to prepare

- Rinse the pig's ears thoroughly in cold running water then dry it using kitchen paper.

- Rub the salt into the ears. Set aside to cure for 6 hours.

- Preheat the water bath to a temperature of 85^{0}C.

- Rinse the pig's ears again, getting rid of as much of the salt as possible, then seal it in a vacuum bag with the oil.

- Place the bag in the water bath and leave to cook for 12 hours. Remove the bag from the bath and set aside to cool.

- Once the ears have cooled to room temperature, remove them from the bag, pat dry and place in the fridge until thoroughly chilled.

- Slice the cold pig's ears into strips 1cm in thickness then sprinkle with a dusting of rice flour.

- Heat some oil to a temperature of 190^0C, then add the pig's ears and fry until crispy. This should take around 2 minutes.

CHAPTER FORTY THREE

SUCKLING PIG WITH CHOU FARCI, HUMMUS AND CHICKPEA FRICASSEE

Ingredients

- 250g of suckling pig loin

- Suckling pig belly

- 250g of suckling pig belly, boned

- 1 sprig of thyme, chopped

- 1 sprig of rosemary, chopped

- salt

Suckling pig sauce

- 1kg suckling pig bones

- 1l chicken stock

- 100g of onion

- 100g of carrots

- 100g of celery

- 100g of leek

- 1 garlic

- 2 sprigs of thyme

- 30g of tomato purée

- 100ml of red wine

- 50g of butter, cubed

Chou farci

- 250g of suckling pig leg, deboned

- 25g of smoked bacon

- 6 savoy cabbage leaves

Pickled onions

- 125ml of white wine vinegar

- 125g of sugar

- 125g of silver skin onion

- 2 black peppercorns

- 1 star anise

- 2 cloves

- 1 bay leaf

Hummus

- 400g of chickpeas
- 3 garlic cloves
- 75ml of olive oil
- 1 tsp smoked paprika
- 3 tsp lemon juice
- 1 tsp sugar
- 125g of tahini
- 1 tsp ground cumin
- salt

Charred leeks

- 2 leeks

Chickpea fricassee

- 100g of chickpeas
- 1 shallot, finely diced
- 1 garlic clove, finely diced
- 1 tsp chopped chives
- 20ml of lemon juice

- 10g of butter

- salt

How to prepare

- To prepare the suckling pig belly, preheat the water bath to a temperature of 85^0C.

- Mix together the salt, chopped thyme and chopped rosemary and massage into the belly.

- Seal the seasoned meat inside a large vacuum bag using a bar sealer.

- Place the bag in the water bath and leave to cook sous vide for 7 hours.

- Unseal the vacuum bag and remove the belly. Pat the meat dry on kitchen paper, then place in a shallow tray lined with baking parchment.

- Cover the meat with another layer of baking parchment and balance a second tray on top.

- Weigh down the top tray with something heavy, then leave to press in the fridge until chilled through.

- Preheat the oven to a temperature of 180^0C/gas mark 4.

- For the suckling pig sauce, place the bones in a roasting dish and cook in the oven until caramelized. This should take approximately 1 hour.

- Heat a splash of oil in a large saucepan, then add the onion, carrot, celery and leek and brown over a high heat.

- When the vegetables are well-colored, stir in the tomato purée, thyme and roasted bones and add enough chicken stock to cover all of the ingredients completely.

- Simmer for 3 hours, pouring in extra stock when necessary to keep the bones covered.

- After this time, strain the sauce through 3 layers of muslin cloth, then place a clean pan and mix in the red wine.

- Cook over a medium heat until reduced to 1/3 of the original volume. When it is ready, the mixture will be sauce-like in consistency.

- Next, make the chou farci. Grind the suckling pig leg and the smoked bacon together in a mincer, then add a splash of the suckling pig sauce and mix well. Keep adding sauce until the mince binds together, then add a pinch of salt and refrigerate for 1 hour.

- After this time, take the meat out of the fridge and divide into 40g pieces. Roll each piece into a ball and arrange on a tray. Place the tray in the fridge and leave to set.

- Bring a saucepan of salted water to the boil and add the cabbage leaves. Simmer for 2 minutes, then remove the leaves and plunge into iced water to halt the cooking process. Leave to drain on kitchen paper.

- Place one of the blanched cabbage leaves on a sheet of cling film and top with a chilled ball of farci. Fold the cabbage over the meat until it is completely encased, then stretch the cling film around the ball to secure the leaf in place.

- Repeat step 15 with rest of the cabbage leaves and meat balls, then place the chou farci in the fridge and leave to set for a minimum of 30 minutes.

- Preheat the water bath to a temperature of 55^{0}C.

- To prepare the sucking pig loin, remove the sinew and chop the meat into 40g slices.

- Seasons the slices with salt, then use a bar sealer to seal each one in a separate vacuum bag with a little oil.

- Place the bags in the water bath and leave to sous vide for 30 minutes.

- Next, pickle the onions. In a large saucepan, combine the water, vinegar, sugar, peppercorns, star anise, cloves and bay leaf. Heat until the liquid boils and the sugar dissolves completely, and then tip the hot mixture over the onions. Set aside until cool.

- When the onions are cool, remove their skins and return them to the pickling liquid. Leave to pickle until needed.

- Preheat the oven to a temperature of 120^{0}C/gas mark 1/4.

- Take the chou farci out of the fridge, remove the cling film and place on a baking sheet in the oven. Cook for 10 minutes, then dip the balls in the suckling pig sauce and leave in a warm place until required.

- For the hummus, mix the chickpeas, garlic cloves, olive oil, paprika, lemon juice, sugar, tahini, cumin and salt in a blender. Add 175ml of hot water and pulse the blender until the mixture becomes smooth.

- To make the charred leeks, fill a saucepan with salted water and bring to the boil. Add the leeks and simmer until they are just cooked. This should take about 5 minutes. Once it is cooked, plunge the leeks into iced water, then leave it on kitchen paper to drain.

- Slice the leeks into 6 equal lengths and put it in hot frying pan. Do not add any oil or cooking fat. Fry the leeks until they are caramelized, then leave in warm place until it is ready to serve.

- Next, make the fricassee. Heat the butter in a small saucepan. When it has completely melted, add the shallot and garlic and sauté over a gentle heat until softened but not colored.

- Mix in the chickpeas and 2 tbsp of the pickled onions. Continue to cook for another 2 minutes, and then add the lemon juice, salt and chives to finish.

- Take the suckling pig belly out of the fridge and take out the weighted tray. Slice the meat into individual portions and place to one side.

- Unseal the vacuum bags containing the suckling pig loin. Take out the meat and pat dry with kitchen paper. At the same time, heat a dash of oil in a frying pan.

- When the oil is hot, add in the loin and caramelize over a medium heat, then set aside to rest, leaving the pan on the heat.

- Arrange the belly slices cut-side down in the hot pan and quickly sear the meat. Turn the slices over and sear the other cut surfaces, then take out from the pan.

- To serve, abundantly smear the base of each plate with hummus and top up with a few spoonfuls of chickpea fricassee. Arrange 1 portion of pork belly, 1 slice of pork loin and 1 ball of chou farci in a line across the centre of the plate, then add 2 pieces of charred leek. Drizzle the warm suckling pig sauce atop the meat and finish the dish with a garnish of puffed pork rind and celery cress.

CHAPTER FORTY FOUR

SOUS VIDE PORK BELLY

Even though it is a relatively cheap cut of meat, pork belly can be succulent and tender if it is treated with care. Low temperatures and long cooking times are important to prevent the meat from drying out and losing its flavor. Pork belly is therefore perfectly suited to being cooked sous vide as this technique allows you to maintain consistently low temperatures over long periods.

Ingredients

- 1kg pork belly

- 2 liters water

- 100g salt

How to prepare

- To ensure even seasoning, brine the pork before cooking. Add the salt to the water and stir until it is dissolved. Put the pork in the water, ensuring that it is totally submerged. Set it aside to brine for 6 hours.

- Preheat the water bath to a temperature of 64°C.

- Take out the pork from the brine, put inside a vacuum bag and seal.

- Place the bag in the water bath and leave it to cook for 24 hours.

- Take the pork out of the bag and pat with kitchen paper to dry, draining off any juices as you do so.

- Move the pork to a tray then put another tray and a heavy weight on top. Rest it in the fridge for a minimum of 6 hours. If possible, leave it overnight.

- Take out the pork from between the two trays and slice it into individual portions. Heat a little oil in a frying pan then add the pork and fry, turning as necessary, until it is crisp and golden on both sides.

CHAPTER FORTY FIVE

PORK SHOULDER WITH HISPI CABBAGE AND APPLES

Ingredients

- 1.4kg pork shoulder

- 14g of salt

Apple and celeriac purée

- 500g of Bramley apple, peeled, cored and sliced

- 25g of olive oil

- 1/2 tsp lemon juice

- 200g of celeriac, peeled and sliced

- 200ml of milk

- 1 pinch of salt

- 1 tsp cider vinegar

Pork sauce

- 1.2kg pork bones

- 800ml of chicken stock

- 400g of pork trimmings

- 400ml of white wine

- 200g of button mushrooms, sliced

- lemon zest, 1 piece

- 1 lemon juice

- 1 garlic clove

- 1 sprig of fresh thyme

- 1.2g of xanthan gum

- 1 tsp Chardonnay vinegar

- 1 pinch of black pepper

Hispi cabbage

- 1 Hispi cabbage

- 10ml of white wine vinegar

- 20ml of duck fat

Red apple slices

- 2 Redlove apples, sliced

- 125ml of lemon juice

- 250ml of water

- 250ml of sugar

How to prepare

- Preheat the water bath to a temperature of 70°C.

- Debone the pork shoulder and rub the salt into meat. Shape the joint into an oblong, then stretch cling film around the meat to make sure it holds the shape. Seal inside a vacuum bag with the use of a chamber sealer.

- Put the bag in the water bath and leave to cook for 12 hours. After this time, move the meat to the fridge and leave it overnight to chill.

- Preheat the water bath to a temperature of 88°C.

- For the apple and celeriac purée, seal the sliced apple and celeriac in a vacuum bag with the olive oil. You will need to use a chamber sealer to do this.

- Put the bag in the water bath and leave it to cook sous vide. After 30 minutes, take out the bag and place the contents in a blender with the lemon juice, milk, salt and cider vinegar. Pulse the mixture in the blender until it is smooth.

- Preheat the oven to a temperature of 180°C/gas mark 4.

- Next, prepare the pork sauce. Arrange the pork bones on a baking tray and place in the oven. Cook it until it is golden brown.

- Heat the chicken stock in a large saucepan. When the stock is boiling, tip the roasted pork bones into the pan and simmer for 1 hour. Put the white wine in a separate saucepan over a medium heat. Cook for 10 minutes, starting the clock when the wine reaches the boil, then set aside until needed.

- Brown the pork trimmings in a big saucepan. When the trimmings have caramelized, empty the meat and fat from the pan into a colander and leave it to drain.

- Pass the stock through a fine sieve to take out the bones, and then place in a clean saucepan with the caramelized trimmings, the button mushrooms and the garlic. Bring to the boil and cook over a gentle heat for 1 hour.

- Strain the sauce through a fine sieve and leave to settle then get rid of any fat that has come to surface. Stir in the xanthan gum to thicken the sauce, add salt and pepper to taste and mix in the lemon juice and vinegar. Infuse the sauce with the thyme sprig and the lemon rind for 20 minutes then set aside until needed.

- Next, prepare the hispi cabbage. Shred the hispi cabbage into long thin strips. Melt the duck fat in a saucepan and add in the cabbage. Sauté until tender, then add salt to season and mix in the vinegar.

- To make the red apple slices, mix the sugar, water and lemon juice in a saucepan. Immerse the apple slices in the mixture and heat until boiling then simmer for 4 minutes. After this time, drain off the liquid and set the apple aside until it is needed.

- For the parsnips, bring a saucepan of salted water to the boil. Add the parsnips and simmer for 3½ minutes.

- Preheat the water bath to a temperature of 62°C.

- Seal the pork shoulder inside a neat vacuum bag using a chamber sealer. Put in the water bath and sous vide for 15 minutes until reheated all the way through. Unseal the bag and pat the meat dry on kitchen paper.

- Put the shoulder skin-side down in a hot frying pan and fry until the skin is crispy. After frying, check that the meat is hot all the way through by inserting a skewer into the centre, then cut into 4 portions.

- To serve, split the hispi cabbage among 4 plates. Heap the cabbage into a pile in the centre of each plate and top with a portion of pork shoulder. Put 2 slices of apple beside the cabbage and dot the plate with apple and celeriac purée. Spoon the pork sauce over the meat and finish each plate with 2 baby parsnips.

CHAPTER FORTY SIX

TEQUILA CHICKEN

Tequila, it makes you happy, oh tequila.......they say that is how the song goes!! A bit cheeky for a Monday tea time but let's see what you think! Try this tasty tequila chicken.

Ingredients

- 2 chicken breast halves, boneless and skinless

- Salt, to taste

- Black pepper, to taste

- 2 tablespoons (10 ml) butter

- 2 tablespoons (10 ml) tequila

- 1 lime, for juice

- Fresh chives, chopped, for garnish

How to prepare

- Fill and preheat your water bath to 63.5C.

- Lightly season the chicken breasts with salt and pepper, place into a small (quart/0.9 liter) food-grade cooking pouch, and vacuum seal.

- Immerse the pouch in the water oven and cook for at least 1 to 1-1/2 hours.

- Remove the pouch from the water oven and the chicken from the pouch. Pat the exterior of the chicken dry with paper towels.

- In a skillet, over high heat, melt the butter and quickly sear the chicken on both sides for color.

- Deglaze the pan with the tequila and scrape up the flavorful brown bits. (For safety, remove the skillet from the heat when adding the tequila to stop flare up.)

- Move the chicken to a warm plate and drizzle with the tequila pan sauce.

- Squeeze on the lime juice and dress up with chopped chives. Enjoy!

CHAPTER FORTY SEVEN

SOUS VIDE CHICKEN WITH ENGLISH MUSTARD AND BROAD BEANS

Ingredients

- 6 chicken thighs, skin on and bone in

- 6 find slices of lemon

- 350g shelled broad beans

- 1 golden onion, finely diced

- 1 tbsp English mustard

- 2 tbsp butter

- 2 tbsp plain flour

- 400mls white wine

- 300mls light chicken or vegetable stock

- 100mls single cream

- Extra virgin olive oil

- Olive oil

- Unsalted butter

- Vegetable oil

- Sea salt

- Black pepper

How to prepare

- Preheat the bath to 66.6°C.

- Season your chicken thighs on both sides with salt and pepper and put them into your vac pouch, then drizzle the lemon slices in extra virgin olive oil and place one on each chicken thigh (non skin side) inside the pouch, then vac seal.

- Put into the water bath for 90 minutes, and when done, remove and chill down until cold inside the pouch and set aside pending when you need them.

- When you're ready to eat, fry the onion in a little olive oil on a medium heat until translucent, then add the knob of butter and when melted, add the flour. Using a whisk mix the flour into the butter, then add the mustard, wine and stock and whisk in until the roux is mixed and begins to thicken, this will take a few minutes. Turn onto a low simmer and stir periodically.

- Take the chicken out of the vac pouch and carefully remove all the meat juices and lemon slices and put them into the mustard sauce, then pat the chicken skin dry with paper towel and season with salt and pepper.

- In a frying pan put a large knob of butter and glug of vegetable oil, and turn onto a high heat. When the butter foams and begins to brown, add the chicken thighs skin side down and do not move once in the pan.

- Cook on the skin side down for 4 to 5 minutes, then season the bare side of the chicken and turn over for another 4 to 5 minutes, while this is happening, add the shelled broad beans and single cream to the mustard sauce to heat through.

- Serve the chicken on top of the mustard sauce with warm baguette and a large glass of vino.

CHAPTER FORTY EIGHT

SOUS VIDE MACKEREL

Mackerel is well-suited to pickling since it has a strong flavor and, as a result, it is not overpowered by the vinegar in the pickle. Pickling food sous vide has a number of advantages over traditional methods. It needs fewer liquid and the food absorbs the flavor of the pickle more rapidly.

Ingredients

- 70ml of white wine vinegar

- 30ml of water

- 30g of sugar

- 3g of salt

- 4 mackerel fillets, pin boned

How to prepare

- Mix the white wine vinegar and the water, and then add the sugar and salt. Stir until totally dissolved.

- Gently lay the mackerel fillets inside a vacuum bag without overlapping them. Add the pickle to the bag and seal.

- Put in the fridge for 30 minutes.

- Once chilled, take the fish out of the bag and gently dry them with kitchen paper.

CHAPTER FORTY NINE

SOUS VIDE SEA BASS

With its firm, nearly meaty flesh and its subtle flavor, sea bass has long been a favorite of many skilled chefs and home cooks. Cooking sous vide is good way to make this popular fish since the use of a sealed vacuum bag locks in moisture and stops drying out.

Ingredients

- 2 sea bass portions, each weighing 120g

- dash of olive oil

- pinch of sea salt

- Preheat the water bath to a temperature of 50°C.

How to prepare

- Sprinkle the sea salt over the sea bass and seal in a vacuum bag with the olive oil.

- Put the bag in the water bath and leave it to cook for 15 minutes. This cooking time is for quite thick portions of sea bass; lessen the time slightly if using thinner pieces.

- Gently slide the cooked fish out the vacuum and pat all over with kitchen paper to dry.

- Lie the fish skin-side down in a very hot frying pan. Sear over a high heat until the skin is crisp and golden then serve immediately

CHAPTER FIFTY

SOUS VIDE BEEF AND PRUNE TAGINE

Ingredients

- 1kg beef shin, cut into cubes

- 2 onions, finely chopped

- 1 pinch of saffron, ground to a powder

- 1 tsp ground ginger

- 1 tsp ground cinnamon

- 1 tsp garlic powder

- 250g of prunes, stoned

- 1 tbsp of runny honey

- 50g of unsalted butter, chilled

- 5 ice cubes

- 1 tbsp of olive oil

- salt

- pepper

How to prepare

- Preheat a water bath to 75°C

- Richly season the diced beef. Heat the oil in a large frying pan and sear the beef in batches, for a couple of minutes, or until it is browned all over. Move the seared meat to a large dish and set it aside

- Decrease the heat under the pan, add the onions and stir occasionally over a low-medium heat for about 10 minutes, or until soft and golden – add a little more oil if needed. Remove the pan from the heat

- Tip away any meat juices that have collected in the dish that the beef has been resting in, or it will be sucked out during vacuum sealing

- Add the onions, saffron, ginger, cinnamon, garlic, prunes and some salt and pepper to the beef and toss thoroughly to evenly distribute the aromatics

- Transfer the meat into a vacuum bag and add the honey, butter and ice cubes

- Vacuum seal the bag and put in the preheated water bath for 12–16 hours

- 10 minutes before you are ready to serve, place the couscous in a bowl and mix through a good pinch of fine sea salt. Add the extra virgin olive oil and add 450ml of hot water from the kettle. Cover up and leave to stand while you dress up the tagine

- Snip the bag open and pour the beef into a large, warmed bowl. Flip through half the toasted almonds and scatter the remaining half over the top, along with the sesame seeds and coriander

- Fluff the couscous with a fork and serve it with the tagine

CHAPTER FIFTY ONE

SPICED PINEAPPLE WITH WHIPPED CREAM CHEESE YOGHURT AND GINGER BISCUITS

This sous vide cooked dessert tastes awesome. Perfect for a family meal or get together.

Ingredients

- 1 x pineapple

- 1 tsp Chinese five spice

- 2 tsp lemon zest

- 1 tsp crushed pink peppercorns

- ¼ tsp nutmeg

- ¼ tsp cinnamon

- 1 tsp allspice

- 200mls white wine

- 100g soft dark brown sugar

Whipped Cream Cheese Yoghurt

- 250 g cream cheese

- 100g natural yoghurt

- 1 ½ tbsp. Vanilla yoghurt

- Grated star anise

- 100g crushed ginger nut biscuits

How to prepare

Spiced pineapple

- Peel the pineapple

- Mix all other ingredients together, place everything under vacuum. Seal and cook sous vide at 85c for 12 hours

Whipped Cream Cheese Yoghurt

- Beat all the ingredients together until it is smooth and silky, set in the fridge overnight

- Build the dish and top with the crushed ginger biscuits

CPSIA information can be obtained
at www.ICGtesting.com
Printed in the USA
BVHW031802020919
557365BV00009B/194/P